ALMIGHTY

ALMIGHTY

How the Most Powerful Being
in the Universe Is Also
Your Loving Heavenly Father

DAVID BUTLER

DESERET
BOOK

Salt Lake City, Utah

FOR DAD—who loves me so liberally—like
a good, good father would.

Library of Congress Cataloging-in-Publication Data
(CIP on file)
ISBN 978-1-62972-451-5

Printed in the United States of America
LSC Communications, Harrisonburg, VA

10 9 8 7 6 5 4 3

INTRODUCTION

I think I turned some heads when I yelled out in the crowded restaurant. It just jumped out of my mouth—a tiny, little yelp.

Strangers are not supposed to grab you. But that's what he did—the man in the crooked black hat. I had just finished paying. One hand was clutching 900 bags of to-go food for my clan, the other was trying to wrangle my wallet back into my pocket, and my eyes were hastily searching for my car keys when he reached across the counter and grabbed my wrist. Like I was a criminal. Fight or flight did not have a chance to kick in before he asked me the question:

"What do you believe?"

What?! I was completely stupefied. This was so bizarre. Why would he be asking me that? Such a random question! Such a personal question.

He must have sensed my confusion. He then tapped my thick white silicone bracelet in response to my puzzled look. The bracelet had been a take-home favor from youth conference. Engraved in big black letters across the band was the phrase "I believe."

He asked again, "So . . . what do you believe?"

"Oh," I stuttered as I searched my mind frantically for the right answer.

You see, the theme of our youth conference had been the thirteenth article of faith, which was clearly too long to fit on the bracelet, so we had settled on an adaptation of the first two words, "We believe." That's what the bracelet referenced, but that wasn't the answer to his question.

I was still so thrown off by the surprise of it all that I fumbled over where to start. My thoughts were a mess. *I believe so many things. What should I say? The whole thirteenth article of faith? Or something else? Where do I begin? What do I pick? Is one truth more important than all the rest? How much does he really want to know? Why is he still holding my wrist? And, for real, where are my car keys?*

The silence wasn't too awkward. My mouth kept stuttering while my mind ran wild, and he just waited patiently with a curious look.

There I was. The stage was set. I was up to bat. This was the opportunity I had been trained for, right? The made-up scenario from seminary was now actually happening. My missionary moment.

I recited the question to myself once more.

"What *do* I believe?"

What do you think you would say if you were me? If you had ten seconds to say just one statement about what you believe, what would it be?

What do you believe?

There is not a *wrong* answer to that question. You believe whatever you choose to believe. There are, however, some truths that are more important than other truths. Wouldn't you agree?

My son Christian is the king of random trivia. If you need a fact that no one on earth needs to know, come talk to him. He knows how fast giraffes run, the number of people that have survived going over Niagara Falls in a barrel, and how many hot dogs Americans eat on average per year. (It's seventy, by the way. That is more than one a week! Lay off the dogs, folks!)

Not all truths are created equal—clearly.

But what about ETERNAL TRUTHS?

Is there ONE

that rises

ABOVE the rest?

I think there is.

During the first general conference of the newly organized Church of Jesus Christ of Latter-day Saints, there was a revelation that was read to those who came, which was known as the Constitution of the Church. You can find it today in section 20 of the Doctrine and Covenants.

The verses in the beginning of the section list some of the amazing miracles that happened in the beginning days of the Church, starting with a fourteen-year-old boy speaking with God in the woods near his home. Then there was a visit from an angel in his bedroom. It talks about the coming forth of the Book of Mormon—a wildly amazing story!

Think of it. An ancient record written on golden tablets in an unknown language that Joseph found buried in a hill just a few short miles from his house. It was translated into English on scraps of paper in borrowed bedrooms at the rapid rate of about six or seven pages per day. This was done by the son of a Vermont farmer and his newfound friends who believed his story and risked everything, in some cases, to help him. And each of them had his or her own marvelous experiences too. Some of them heard the voice of God and visited with angels and saw miraculous, marvelous things. Those were the beginning days of a frontier church that now fills the world.

Can you picture the people who were there at that first general conference as the story was retold for everyone? Some of them with tears in their eyes and sacred memories replaying in their minds; others nodding to each other as they heard mentions of the spectacular experiences that had occurred since the First Vision. What a day! What a beginning!

And then in the revelation, the Lord said this:

"BY THESE THINGS WE KNOW . . ."

What things? The marvelous and wonderful events surrounding the Restoration of Christ's Church on the earth. The angels. The visits. The revelations. The miracles. All of "these things."

"By these things we know that there is a God in heaven, who is infinite and eternal, from everlasting to everlasting the same unchangeable God, the framer of heaven and earth, and all things which are in them" (D&C 20:17).

So many good things have dominoed from Joseph Smith's visit to the Sacred Grove. But above all else, the miracles of the Restoration prove, first and foremost, that there is a God in heaven.

That seems to be number one. A golden truth.

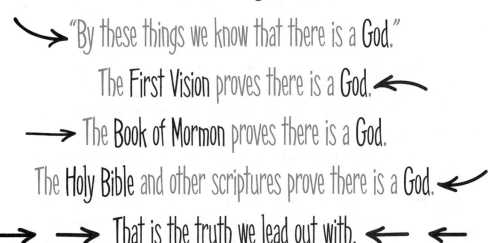

"By these things we know that there is a God."

The First Vision proves there is a God.

The Book of Mormon proves there is a God.

The Holy Bible and other scriptures prove there is a God.

That is the truth we lead out with.

"We believe in God, the Eternal Father, and in His Son, Jesus Christ, and in the Holy Ghost" (Articles of Faith 1:1).

This supernal and sublime truth gives meaning, power, and significance to every other truth we believe and proclaim to the world. It is first and most important. It is what we believe.

So if I could redo my life, I think when the hand-grabber with the black hat in the Cheesecake Factory asked me what I believed, I would say something like this:

"Sir, I believe in a lot of things. But above all else,

I BELIEVE IN GOD."

1

ALMIGHTY GOD
THE LOVE OF A FATHER

In my phone, one of my most favorite friends is listed in my contacts as "Stix." That's not his real name. His real name is Trevor. But I call him Stix because of how much he loves stickers. You should see his door—it is covered in them! It's my favorite part of his house. Scroll through more of my contacts and you would see that I also have a Jack Attack, a Loopy, a Cheat, a Bruiser, a Caterpillar, a Ty-Bo, a Daisy, a Cookie, a Tips, a Mr. Morning, a Snickers, a Grizz, and a Bing Bong. Again, not any of their real names. Each of their nicknames has a story behind it—something the person said, something he or she loves, or just a random experience we had together.

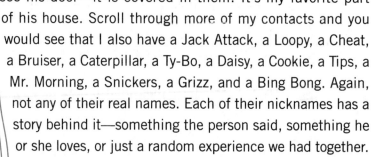

A lot of names are like this—including nicknames *and* real names. Parents sometimes name their kids after someone they want to honor or give them names that have special meanings.

Does your name have a meaning or story?

Names throughout the scriptures and in ancient cultures were very important. They weren't just labels but descriptions of who that person was. That is especially true of the names of God.

Throughout scripture, He has many names and titles.[1] Each of them teaches us something about who He is and His relationship to us. Let's look at a few.

God

God itself is a title. This title refers to a being that we follow, worship, look to, and love. When we use the name *God*, we are usually speaking about the supreme Governor of the universe and the Father of mankind (see Mosiah 4:9; D&C 109:77).

Lord

Lord means leader, master, ruler, or commander. The title is given to someone who is in charge of looking after, watching over, and taking care of others, so it is perfect for God. He is one who leads and oversees. He has perspective, wisdom, and answers. We can counsel with Him. It is a title of deep respect and honor. It refers to Him as a loving master over His creations (have a look at Alma 37:37).

Almighty

Almighty is a name that shows all power and ultimate control. No person or other influence is ever above Him. He can do anything, anytime, anywhere. He is omniscient, which means He knows all. He is also omnipotent, which means He has unlimited power (check out Alma 26:35).

Endless

Endless is a name of God. It means that He will always be. He will never leave. His existence and His love will never expire. He is everlasting (you might want to read Moses 1:3; Moroni 7:22).

⟶ The Lord Thy God ⟵

Sometimes a combination of other titles is used to remind us that He is all of these things. Also, and perhaps more importantly, the word *thy* shows us that He is not just *a* God, but He is *your* God. You have claim on each other. There is a relationship there (these scriptures are so good: Deuteronomy 30:9–10; D&C 132:2).

⟶ I Am That I Am ⟵

This is a phrase that comes from Hebrew and is one of God's names. In another translation, it means, "I am who I will always be." Who God was in the past is who He will be forever. He is trustworthy and He is unchanging. He is the same yesterday, today, and forever (explore Exodus 3:14–15; D&C 20:12).

⟶ Father ⟵

This is the title that He is most often referred to by, and perhaps His favorite. He wants us to know that He is not just powerful, but that He is our father. Not a boss or a government ruler, but a dad. Your dad (you will love this one: Acts 17:28–29).

Which name or title of God means the most to you?
(It can be one listed here or another you love.)

The name I love most	Why I love it

God the Father rules and reigns supreme over everything in the universe. He came before everything we know. He has all power. He has all wisdom and understanding. There is not anything in this world—past, present, or future—that God does not know about or that is too big for Him to handle. He watches over all. He cares about all. He is involved in all things. He is the source of all strength, wisdom, goodness, and love that can be found in any person, place, or thing in all of existence. Our Father is God above and over all. HE CAN DO ANYTHING, ANYTIME, ANYWHERE. That is what His names teach us.

Many, many years ago, there was a showdown in the desert between Moses and Satan. It might seem intimidating to come face to face with the devil, but only moments before, Moses had stood face to face with Jehovah, who spoke to Moses on behalf of God the Father. And in that conversation with God, Moses learned truths that gave him strength against the devil—strength that would carry him through the rest of his life. The same truth and strength has the ability to lift and carry all of us.

"And God spake unto Moses, saying: Behold, I am the LORD GOD ALMIGHTY, and ENDLESS is my name; for I am without beginning of days or end of years; . . . And behold, THOU ART MY SON. . . . And I have a work for thee, Moses, MY SON; . . . there is no God beside me, and all things are present with me, for I know them all" (Moses 1:3–6; emphasis added).

The Lord then peeled back eternity and let Moses have a peek. He had just seen a glimpse of God's creations and power, but when it was over, Moses fainted and lay on the ground passed out for several hours. The magnitude of it was overwhelming! When Moses finally regained his strength, he concluded, "Now . . . I know that man is nothing, which thing I never had supposed" (Moses 1:10).

Moses had been raised in Egypt, the ancient world power. Without Google Earth to help him see, he had probably imagined that the pyramids were the center of the universe and that he was playing a big part in it as royalty in Pharaoh's court. He would have naturally assumed that Egypt was a big deal. Now he was realizing the truth.

He was SMALLER than he ever knew, and God was BIGGER than he ever imagined.

Moses fainted at the thought of how small he was compared to God. And that is a truth worth remembering. It is important to let it settle in our hearts. God really is much BIGGER and more POWERFUL than we know. And yet, as Moses sat there feeling quite small, I can imagine that he must have remembered that just moments before, God, the greatest of all, had been there with him—perhaps sitting down on a rock right next to him. This great, grand, almighty, end-less Lord and God took the time to teach Moses, His son. In all of His power and glory and creations and might, in that moment, His heart and attention were centered on one of His children. He always has time for the one.

GOD IS BIG,
BUT NOT
TOO BIG FOR
MOSES.

AND NOT
TOO BIG
FOR YOU.

And then after Moses arose, the devil arrived, trying to show off his power and tempting Moses to follow and worship him.

And Moses responded with truth—A POWERFUL TRUTH.

"And it came to pass that Moses looked upon Satan and said: Who art thou?

For behold,

I AM A SON OF GOD"

(Moses 1:13).

Moses knew the power of God. He had just witnessed His glory and strength. And he knew what he meant to God—he was His son. So he dismissed the devil, who then threw a bit of a temper tantrum before leaving (see Moses 1:19–21).

"And calling upon the name of God, he beheld his glory again, for it was upon him; and he heard a voice, saying: Blessed art thou, Moses, for I, THE ALMIGHTY, HAVE CHOSEN THEE. . . . And lo, I am with thee, even unto the end of thy days" (Moses 1:25–26).

God the Almighty chose Moses and called him out by name. There on the mountain, He promised Moses He would always be with him. Who God was with Moses is who He will be for you, too. He is just as almighty and just as full of glory today as He was when He spoke on that mountaintop. He thinks of you, has time for you, has a work for you, will watch over you, and is willing and ready to be with you even until the end of days. All we need to do is to call on Him. And just as He told Moses, He is your father, and you are His daughter or son.

```
┌─────────────────────────────────────┐
│           MY NAME IS                  │
│                                       │
│   _____     │
│                                       │
│           AND I AM A                  │
│   CHILD OF THE LIVING GOD.            │
└─────────────────────────────────────┘
```

The title of *Father* is not just a fancy word or poetry; it is a reality. Heavenly Father is exactly that. He is our Father who lives in heaven. He has a dad's heart and love for you. All over the world, children grow up singing the song "I Am a Child of God," and they are absolutely right.

We are not just His creations—

WE ARE
>>> HIS <<<
CHILDREN

—as literally as we are children of our parents here on earth. But He is different than our earthly fathers. Some of us were lucky enough to be born to earthly parents who have some of the same characteristics as our Heavenly Father. Others of us were not so lucky. But whatever the situation may be in our earthly home, we all share the wonder and the glory of coming from a heavenly home with exalted, glorified, and almighty Heavenly Parents who adore us. You really are Their little girl or little boy.

Have you ever heard or used the word SOVEREIGN before? The word *sovereign* is often used to describe kings and queens. It means that they are the head authority and have the most influence and power on all issues in their kingdom.

This is true of God in the universe. The Father is a sovereign ruler with supreme and ultimate power. Often we refer to God as a king who reigns over His kingdom—THE KINGDOM OF GOD. But who and what does God rule over? What is His kingdom? The answer is: US. HIS FAMILY. So a synonym for "kingdom of God" is "the family of God." And who is the head of a family? Parents. A father and a mother. This is the government of the universe.

An exalted father and mother who rule and reign over their family.

You will notice I started using the phrases "parents" and "mother." We have a Heavenly Mother. She is an exalted Queen and our literal mother. Although we do not know as much about Her and Her role, it is important to know She is there, loves us, and rules and reigns with the Father over their family—us.

Every word He speaks, every action He takes, and every thought He has is motivated by and born out of the love He has in His father heart. You can take that as a guarantee every single time. Even the trials we experience on a daily basis, the evil that exists because He gives us agency, the times He chooses not to answer our prayers the way we asked, and even His punishment and justice are evidence of a loving God. Whenever you read about Him in the scriptures or watch Him moving in your own life, you can always assume and look for His love to be present. Eventually you will find it. HIS LOVE IS ALWAYS THERE.

And do you want to know something?

HIS LOVE IS FREE.

He loves you right where you are,

RIGHT AS YOU ARE,

no matter who you are.

REALLY.

In this book we are going to explore several of the ways that God shows that love to us—especially in those times when it feels like He doesn't. We will talk about the way we recognize and receive that love and what we do because of it. But here at the beginning, I want you to be certain that I know for a fact that anyone reading this book is loved by God as much as anyone else reading it. You don't earn his love. You do not need to reach a certain level before it kicks in.

It is

always

there.

ALWAYS AVAILABLE.

That love can change us, motivate us to do things, give us peace, give us strength, and give us power and purpose. The love of the Father is what gives light and life and meaning to everything. We'll talk more about this later, but let's first explore more about God's love for us.

✭ God is Almighty.

HE IS LORD. ♡

♔ HE IS SOVEREIGN.

HE IS ENDLESS. ✩

♥ He is our Father.

And all of His wisdom, power, might, authority, and everlasting influence
♡ are used to show His cherished children His love.

GOD **IS** LOVE. ♡
THAT IS ONE OF HIS NAMES.

AND YOU ARE HIS CHILD. ♥

2

"FOR GOD SO LOVED THE WORLD"

God Showed Us Love By Sending Jesus

If this book had photographs, I would put a full-page, full-color photo of me hiking through the Alps wearing my brother-in-law's authentic German lederhosen outfit. Red-and-white checkered shirt, elk-skin pants with decorated suspenders, Pinocchio-style hat, high socks, and brown suede clogging shoes. I had it all. If you found that outfit in your brother-in-law's closet, and you were in the Alps, you would have done it too! I looked like a local. Or maybe more like one of those creepy dolls from the "It's a Small World" ride at Disneyland. Either way, I looked legit.

Last summer, my wife Jenny and I took a trip to see her sister's family in Austria. You should put visiting that country on your bucket list. It is absolutely stunning! Towering mountain peaks overlooking green pastures and valleys echoing with the clanging of bells that hang from the necks of the happiest cows in the world. A dream land. As part of our adventures, we took trams high up into the peaks of the Austrian Alps to hike around. While planning the trip several months before, I texted my brother-in-law to tell him that the only thing I wanted to do while I was in Austria was go to the top of a mountain to find and pick an edelweiss flower.

The edelweiss is a flower with velvety white petals and a yellow center. It only grows high, high in the Alps on the edges of rocky cliff sides. They are rare to find and very dangerous to pick. In fact, my brother-in-law told me that in all his years living there, he had never seen one growing in the wild. For centuries, brave German and Austrian boys had hiked high above the clouds and scaled the cliffs to find and pick edelweiss flowers for girls that they fancied. Anyone could buy sunflowers or daisies from the local markets, but picking an edelweiss took sacrifice and risk.

IT WAS A TRUE Gift of LOVE.

I have always wanted to pick an edelweiss flower. Every night, when I tuck my kids into bed, I sing them the edelweiss song from the movie *The Sound of Music*. I have been slightly obsessed with these flowers for over a decade.

The moment I spotted a small patch of them about ten yards down the cliff side, I knew I had to get one. It was my dream come true! And I had Jenny there with me. It was meant to be! Slowly, carefully, and very foolishly, I scaled down the loose rocks, gripping grass patches and crumbling dirt clods until finally the flowers were almost within reach. I stretched my arm out as far as I could and tickled the stem with my fingertips, careful not to look down, and more careful not to fall down the 300-foot drop of death.

As I am typing this memory, my hands are sweating and my heart is racing, but I am happy to report that the edelweiss flower from that particular cliff is now framed on our bedroom wall as evidence that I not only lived but was victorious in my death-defying act of bravery for my lady love! Jenny was furious, and my blood pressure did not go down until dinner that night, but I got my prize! And I also got a reluctant kiss on the cheek at the top of one of the highest peaks in Austria.

The edelweiss flower is unique and special because of the cost required to give one. Long ago, there were no trams, no guardrails, and no tourists walking around on the tops of these mountains. Picking an edelweiss showed a dedication and love that no other flower could show. Yes, there were other brave acts and gifts of love that a boy could give a girl, but the best of them all was picking an edelweiss.

It might be my legal and moral obligation to tell you not to try these types of things at home. They were performed by a professional.

What is the nicest thing anyone has ever done for you?

_____

_____

_____

God has so many ways that He shows us His love. His devotion and dedication to us can be seen all around. Every chapter of this book shows an aspect of that love. Instead of saving the best for last, I decided to lead out with it. God's most profound and complete way of showing His love to us is found in the central message of the scriptures.

> # "For God so loved the world, that he gave his only begotten Son"
> ## (John 3:16).

God is the giver of all good gifts. He is the best gift giver in the universe. When He wanted to show His love to us in the most perfect way, He showed it by sending His Son. He did not give us a blank check, a gift card, or the newest iPhone. HE GAVE A CHILD—HIS MOST PRIZED POSSESSION. And it cost Him dearly.

Several years ago I was talking with a friend of mine about God and other heavenly things. He told me, surprisingly, that he didn't think that he had ever felt the love of God. Frankly, I was a little surprised. I was so puzzled by that statement. I told him that those feelings were very different from the experiences I was having and that I simply did not know what to say in response. I could not figure out how someone could not see and feel how much God loves him. It was just a foreign idea to me.

There are, however, people that feel this way. My friend was not lying to me. He had sincere eyes. And even though I think sin can prevent a person from accepting or recognizing God's love, I do NOT think that everyone who struggles with the concept of God's love is struggling *because* of sin. There are many other reasons.

As a side note to that comment—God loves sinners, too. We should ALL be happy about that, because we all fall into that camp. We are all sinners! But God loves even those caught up in big sins. I have taught some seminary lessons in the youth prison a few times, and I want you to know that they have been some of the most spiritual experiences of my life. It was unexpected, but in those moments it was as if God let me see those boys the way He sees them. It absolutely blew me away. Those hours behind bars are sacred memories to me.

GOD LOVES ALL Of HiS CHiLDREN!

But back to my friend. What if you or someone you know cannot feel or recognize God's love? Is there anyone you know like that? Have you ever struggled with it? Have you ever been certain that God loves others but were unsure about yourself?

WELL, LET ME TELL YOU SOMETHiNG.

I DO NOT NEED TO MEET YOU
(although I wish I could)
TO KNOW THAT YOU ARE LOVED, LOVED, LOVED BY GOD.

BECAUSE I HAVE EVIDENCE Of iT.

The greatest evidence I have that He loves you is the same evidence I have that He loves me.

AND THAT IS
JESUS CHRIST.

Every one of God's creations, His words, and His actions are evidences of His care and compassion, but Jesus Christ is Heavenly Father's greatest, most precious, most important way to show you and me that He is 100% invested in us and loves us without reservation. When you picture Jesus suffering in the olive tree garden or hanging on the cross at Calvary, you are witnessing what God feels about you. He loved you so passionately, and wanted you to have everything He has so desperately, that He sent His perfect, beautiful Son to the world to die for you. The Father of us all arranged for and allowed this to happen because of love. THAT was His motivation.

It was the motivation for the giving **Father** and the sacrificing **Son**.

They **both** went in **willingly**.

They **both** went in because of **love**.

No matter what else happens in this life, that event—

JESUS COMING

TO THE WORLD

AND DYING

FOR YOU

—is your best
and greatest evidence
that God loves you.

"For God SO LOVED THE WORLD,* that he gave his ONLY begotten SON" (John 3:16).

*THIS MEANS YOU.

Sometimes, when we're reading the scriptures, it can be difficult to know whether we are reading about or hearing the words of Heavenly Father or of Jesus Christ. When prophets preach and teach about Them, it can also be difficult to know which of Them they are prophesying about. Titles and names like *God, Lord*, and even *Father* can be used to describe either of Them. There are a few reasons for this difficulty and overlap.

One of the main reasons is because

JESUS CHRIST
REPRESENTS
THE FATHER
TO THE WORLD.

Rarely do we hear the voice of or see the Father appearing in the scriptures. More than nine times out of ten, Heavenly Father sends Jesus Christ to speak and act for Him. In fact, there are only a handful of times in scripture when we are certain that we hear the actual voice of the Father or see Him with His Son. These include at the baptism of Jesus (see Matthew 3:16), during the appearance of Jesus to the Nephites (see 3 Nephi 11:7), and in the Sacred Grove with Joseph Smith (see JS–H 1:17). On each of these occasions, the Father spoke, but notice that it was always to introduce and bear witness of His Son. On all other occasions that are recorded, the Father sent Jesus to speak and act for Him.

As Jesus was gathered with His Apostles in an upper room in Jerusalem, Philip, one of His disciples, requested of Jesus to "shew us the Father." He wondered when Jesus would take them to meet the Father. The Savior's answer taught this powerful truth:

"Have I been so long time with you, and yet hast thou not known me, Philip? he that hath seen me hath seen the Father" (John 14:8–9).

"Oh, Philip," He seemed to tenderly reply. "Have we been together this long and you haven't figured it out yet? When someone has met me they essentially have met the Father."

Everything Jesus came and did while He was on the earth was to show us the character and nature of God the Father.

EVERY MIRACLE, EVERY MESSAGE, AND EVERY MOMENT WAS A MANIFESTATION OF THE HEART OF BOTH OF THEM.

————————→

Jesus is kind. So is God the Father. Jesus is merciful, and so is God the Father. Jesus is powerful, and so is God the Father. When we see the tenderness of Jesus, we see the tenderness of the Father. Jesus inherited all of His goodness, power, and divinity from the Father. God the Father sent Him to show us how He feels about us. He sent Jesus to speak His love to us and also as a gift of love *for* us.

GOD THE FATHER AND JESUS CHRIST ARE SEPARATE BEINGS. HOWEVER, THEY ARE MORE ONE THAN THEY ARE SEPARATE. THEY ARE ONE IN PURPOSE, MISSION, CHARACTER, AND LOVE. PERFECTLY UNITED. THEY DO HAVE THEIR DIFFERENT ROLES IN THE PLAN OF SALVATION, BUT THEY ACT TOGETHER TO SAVE AND LOVE THE HUMAN FAMILY.

In all ways, especially in His great atoning sacrifice, death, and Resurrection, Jesus was sent to show the world the love of the Father.

God shows us His love in countless ways, but Jesus was and is Heavenly Father's edelweiss—His greatest gift of love that required the ultimate sacrifice.

Do you know someone who struggles with knowing whether God loves him or her? Go **mark or tag** the verse John 3:16 in your scriptures or on your phone so you have it ready to **share with someone who needs it**. Perhaps there is someone you could share it with today. No matter what our circumstances in life are, the trials and disappointments we experience, or the things that don't go our way, we all can be certain that **God loves us** because He sent His Son.

3

THE GIFT GIVER
God Shows Us Love through the Holy Ghost

I hate goodbyes. When I talk to people on the phone, I have to wait for them to hang up first. I constantly overstay my welcome at friends' houses and am usually the last one to leave our family Sunday night dinner every week. Despite the fact that I moved away from home over fifteen years ago, I still choke back tears and feel a lump in my throat every time I leave my parents' house after a trip to Texas. As a seminary teacher, I have gotten close to a handful of students who have then left on missions. Those are my best and also my hardest days. Goodbyes are not my thing. I think I am just addicted to being with people, because I also do not like a lot of alone time. I don't like to drive alone or eat alone, and I could never in ten million years go to a movie all by myself. It is not in my DNA.

This is probably why I have always been both crushed and comforted by the goodbyes that happen between Jesus and His Apostles in John chapter 14. They had been together for three years before this Last Supper—walking, talking, sharing, loving, and ministering together full-time. They must have all been extremely close with each other. AND THEN JESUS HAD TO GO. He hinted at it early on and told them directly later in His life that He would one day have to leave them. They didn't understand it. Perhaps they didn't want to believe that He would ever leave.

As sad as that was, before He left, Jesus gave His Apostles this magnificent promise:

"And I will pray the Father, and he shall give you another Comforter, that he may abide with you for ever; even the Spirit of truth; . . . ye know him; for he dwelleth with you, and shall be in you" (John 14:16–17).

"You will never be alone," He told them. "The Father will send you a Comforter." That Comforter is the Holy Ghost. God sends the Holy Ghost to us as a gift of His love.

The Holy Ghost is the third member of the Godhead. He shares the same character and attributes as the Father and the Son. He is one with Them in purpose and plan. He loves you and me with the love of the Father. When you feel His presence, you are also feeling the presence of the Father and the Son. When people say, "I felt the Spirit with me," they could just as easily say, "I felt God with me."

One of the major differences between the Father and the Son and the Holy Ghost is in Their physical form. Heavenly Father and Jesus Christ both have resurrected and perfected, immortal, eternal bodies of flesh and bone. The Holy Ghost does not, "but is a personage of Spirit. Were it not so, the Holy Ghost could not dwell in us" (D&C 130:22).

Because He can dwell in us,

the Holy Ghost is the member of the Godhead that connects us to the Father and the Son while we are away from Them.

He testifies to us of Their existence, Their love, and Their goodness. In fact, when you feel the love of the Father, it is most often the Holy Ghost who has delivered that feeling to your heart. When we are making decisions, HE iS AVAiLABLE. When we are lonely, HE CAN BE WiTH US. When we need help, support, and strength, HE iS WiLLiNG TO BE THERE. The Father, through the Holy Ghost, wants to guide us in choosing happy lives and helps us remember the truths and holy memories we have experienced. Somehow, the Spirit has a way to ease the homesickness we all have for heaven and can fill our hearts with joy. He is God's messenger of love and grace during all hours of our journey on earth. In a way we do not fully understand, He delivers the forgiving and cleansing power of the Savior's Atonement to us as well.

WHEN OUR FATHER iN HEAVEN WANTS TO MAKE A PERSONAL CONNECTiON WiTH OUR SOULS, HE OFTEN MAKES THAT CONNECTiON THROUGH THE MiSSiON AND MiNiSTRY OF THE HOLY GHOST.

Not only did Jesus have to leave His disciples during New Testament times; each of us also had to say goodbye to our Heavenly Parents when we came down to this earth. We are going to talk more about our Father's plan for us in a later chapter, but part of it included being separated from Him. Part of it included goodbyes.

Here on earth, we experience a lot of painful and troubling things. We have doubts, fears, sicknesses, temptations, and weaknesses. We wrestle against the devil and the natural man. Our Heavenly Father knew this would be the case. Because He loves us, He sent us a Comforter—the Holy Ghost. The gift of the Holy Ghost is the most precious gift we can receive and enjoy while we are on this earth. For those who choose to live with that privilege,

it is literally the GIFT of constant companionship of a member of the GODHEAD.

In addition to that amazing gift—the personal companionship of the Holy Ghost—the Father sends other gifts to the world through the ministry of the Spirit.

There is a scene in the book *The Lion, the Witch and the Wardrobe*, by C. S. Lewis, that illustrates another one of the ways God shows this love through the Holy Spirit. For those who have not read the book or seen the movie, the land of Narnia, a mystical place you can only visit by entering in through a magic wardrobe, is in an eternal winter. A witch rules the land with fear and hopelessness and hatred and is trying to banish all warmth, light, and goodness. Four children, Peter, Susan, Edmund, and Lucy, stumble into Narnia and soon learn they are a part of a prophecy that they will be leaders in a battle against the evil witch and will restore the land back to its glory days before her reign.

As the children are traveling through the snow fields of Narnia, running from the witch and her pack of soldier wolves, they come across an unexpected visitor—Santa Claus! He rides in laughing on his jingling golden sled with his bag of gifts. He gives each of the children a present—a weapon or instrument to use in the battle they will soon face. To Peter, a sword with a hilt of gold and a shield with the emblem of a lion. To Susan, a bow, a quiver full of arrows, and a horn to blow in times of trouble. To little Lucy, a bottle of the juice from fire flowers—one drop could heal any injury. Each was a gift of wonder and great value, and each of them would be essential in their battle against the White Witch.

C. S. Lewis wrote his Narnia books as parables about the battle we fight in life. Many people recognize Santa in this scene as representing the Holy Ghost—the giver of gifts.

We do not battle against a witch and winter, but we are battling while we are here on this earth.

Satan has been waging a war against God and those who follow Him since before we were born. That battle still continues. And

the Father never intended us to fight all on our own.

He loves us desperately and wants us to be victorious!

Heavenly Father sends the Holy Ghost to deliver gifts of wonder and great value to each of us. These are called "spiritual gifts." They are designed to help us in our battles. Some of them include the gift of faith, the gift to believe, the gift to be healed, the gift to heal, and the gift of charity. Through the ministry of the Spirit, the Father is able not only to connect with us but to give us the additional strengths, powers, and attributes we will need to thrive here on earth. When we are weak, He can send us the gift of endurance. When we are annoyed, He can send us the gift of patience. When we are lonely, He can send us the gift of companionship. When we cannot think of the words to say, He can send us the gift of tongues. The scriptures list a few of the spiritual gifts the Father sends, but there are so many more. There are gifts for dealing with every situation. His gifts are exactly what we need in our unique and individual circumstances. All we need to do is ask. Some of them are given immediately, and others He helps us develop throughout our life. He really is the best gift giver.

What special gift or extra blessing do you need in your life battle right now?
Have you asked for it?
What gifts have you seen flow into your life from God? Have you received strength? forgiveness? humility?

A few years ago, I had to say goodbye to one of my dearest friends and heroes, my grandpa, "Pom Pom." As many of you have experienced, saying goodbye to loved ones as they go back to heaven is one of the hardest parts of life. Not too long after my grandpa died, my grandma gave me one of his ties. It was a yellow one that he wore on special occasions. It is such a happy tie, and to me it represents his jolly nature and the very joyful and sacred memories that we shared while he was still here. Whenever I have something hard to do or am involved in a special occasion of my own— at church, or at work, or wherever—I wear Pom Pom's tie. In a way, it makes me feel connected to him. On the days I wear it, before I walk out the front door, I lift it up for my wife and kids to see and then remind them, "Pom Pom is coming with me today." It makes me feel like I am not doing the hard thing alone. I feel like I have my hero with me.

In a far more profound way, our Father in Heaven stays connected to us through the Holy Ghost. He whispers, warns, sanctifies, settles, guides, and gives gifts through Him and by Him. AND ABOVE ALL, WE ARE NEVER, EVER ALONE! No father, especially one as good as ours, would send his children away without a way to reach them at any time, any place, and in any way he needed or wanted to. Our Father's gift giving never ends. In a way, it is Christmas morning every day.

4

BECOME

God Shows Us Love by providing a Plan

There were so many reasons I loved teaching Steve and his family while I was a missionary in Korea. The first reason was that he was from Australia. So he spoke English! For a new missionary who still couldn't ask where the bathroom was in Korean, it felt like I won the lottery when we met their family and I could teach them in my own language. However, the top reason I remember our lessons together so clearly is because of what Steve helped me discover about God.

One afternoon, we were at Steve's house teaching his family about the plan of salvation. I had a piece of paper out on his desk and was drawing circles that represented the premortal life, earth, the spirit world, and the kingdoms of glory. I was teaching them about the great questions of where we came from, why we are here, and where we are going after this life. While talking about life on earth, I taught that we are here trying to return to the presence of our Heavenly Father. Then Steve stopped me dead in my tracks with a question that stumped me.

"Wait a minute," he said. "Did you just tell me I lived with God before I was born?"

"Yes!" I answered enthusiastically.

"And I was happy there?" he clarified.

"Absolutely," I said back.

"And you just said that while we are on earth, we are trying to return to live with God again?" he asked as a follow-up question.

"Yes, sir," I beamed back.

"Well," Steve said with some hesitancy, "if we already lived with God and were happy, then why would God send us away just to see if we could make it back? I mean, if we were already happy and with God, why even have this middle circle at all? Why come to earth?"

I thought about it for a second and could not think of much to say. I had grown up my whole life singing the phrase, "Teach me all that I must do TO LIVE WITH HIM SOMEDAY."[2] But Steve was right. I had already lived with Him. And I had been happy. So why send me away?

Now that I am a dad, I understand Steve's confusion even more. Could you imagine if I loaded all of my kids into the car, drove them to a park in a distant state, dropped them off, and then rolled down my window to explain they needed to find their own way back?

"But, Dad," they would say, "why are you dropping us off so far from home?"

"Well . . . to see if you can make it back, kids. To live with me again."

"But we already live with you."

"I know," would be my reply. "But this is just part of the plan."

"But we could die out here—get hit by a truck or eaten by a bear."

"Well, that is just part of the risk, kids. Good luck!"

Can you even imagine? Dads don't do that. Well, some might, but good dads do not do that, and

OUR FATHER IN HEAVEN IS A GOOD, GOOD FATHER

I was stumped. I could not figure out why we needed to come to the earth. I knew we needed to receive a physical body, but it had to be more than that. He could just give us a body, right? All of a sudden, God became irrational and unfair in my mind. WHY WOULD HE DO SOMETHING LIKE THIS? Often in Sunday School I had heard people say that this life was a test. But why would God want to test us to see if we can live with Him? Dads don't seem to do that either. There was something I was missing.

> Have you ever thought through this? Why would God send us away? What reason would a loving Father have to send His children away from home?

For the next few weeks, I studied and prayed and pondered and asked others about Steve's question. I felt a responsibility as a missionary to get him the answer, but I was more motivated to figure it out for myself. There had to be more to life than just returning to live with God. Yes, we were separated, and yes, I wanted to return to live with Him, but that did not explain WHY we got separated in the first place. Why would my loving Father ever send me away? The reason could not be to prove to Him that I was worthy to live with Him. I had already been there. And He already loved me.

One morning while I was doing my scripture study, I came across a verse in the book of Moses that I had studied in seminary. I remember memorizing it while riding in the back of my aunt's Suburban the summer before my freshman year. She was a seminary teacher and was trying to get me a head start on the upcoming year. The verse is Moses 1:39. It is not a very long verse, but it might be one of the most helpful verses I know of in the scriptures.

The verse comes as part of that conversation between Moses and God on the high mountain peak that we already talked about. Remember when God showed Moses a portion of His creations? Moses wanted to know W H Y. Why did He do all the things that He did? What was His purpose behind all of it? The answer came in that little verse I memorized.

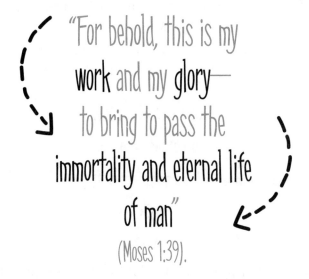

"For behold, this is my work and my glory— to bring to pass the immortality and eternal life of man" (Moses 1:39).

This is His plan. This is His purpose. His work and His glory is to bring to pass, or bring about, the immortality and eternal life of His children. It is what He is working toward 24/7.

Immortality means to live forever. To never die. That is one of God's purposes and plans—for us to live forever in resurrected bodies. The other of His purposes is to help us receive eternal life. Unless someone is familiar with scriptural vocabulary, *eternal life* sounds a lot like *immortality*. It sounds like another way to say "living forever." But it means so much more.

The phrase *eternal life* in scripture means not only living forever WITH God, but living forever LIKE God. Eternal, or Endless, is one of God's names. So

ETERNAL LIFE MEANS "GOD'S LIFE,"

or life like God.

We talked about a simple truth in chapter one, and God said it to Moses on the mountaintop. We are children of God. As His children, we have a divine potential. We inherited from our Heavenly Parents the ability and potential to become like Them.

Our Heavenly Father did not just want us
TO LIVE WITH HIM;
He wanted us
TO LIVE LIKE HIM.

He is the happiest Being in all of the universe, and He wanted *us* to share with Him in what He has and how He lives.

All my life I just figured that
God wanted me to live with Him
—and He does! He misses us so desperately.

But He would not
have sent us away

unless He had something bigger
—something much, much bigger—
in mind.
And He does!

GOD SENT US HERE ON PURPOSE
AND WITH A PURPOSE.

The great purpose God has for each of us is to help us become like Him so that we can enjoy the kind of life He enjoys.

President Joseph F. Smith taught, "Man, as a spirit, was begotten and born of heavenly parents, and reared to maturity in the eternal mansions of the Father, prior to coming upon the earth in a temporal [physical] body."[3] We all wish we could remember the days in those mansions before we were born. And one day we will! We lived with our Father and Mother in Heaven before we came to this world. They are exalted and perfected Beings filled with holiness and with love. They raised us as spirit children before we ever came here. They were different from us, and there were aspects to Their lives that we wished we could have. The Father's plan provided a way for that to be possible.

In what ways were we different from our Heavenly Parents in the premortal world?

_____

_____

_____

_____

_____

Let's discuss a few ways that we were different from our Heavenly Parents. One of those aspects was THEIR FAMILY. When we gathered all together to hear our Father's plan in the pre-mortal world, we gathered as a family. I imagine our loving Father stood next to our loving Mother, and together we stood near them as sons and daughters in one big family.

We yearned for the chance to start families of our own. President Dallin H. Oaks taught,

"Our theology begins with heavenly parents. Our highest aspiration is to be like them."[4] Our Father and Mother sent us to earth to have the experience of choosing a spouse and together having children and raising them like our Heavenly Parents raised us.

Another one of the differences between us and our Heavenly Parents was THEIR BODIES. They had glorified, celestial, resurrected bodies. In a way that we do not quite understand, the perfect uniting of our spirits and our bodies through the Resurrection allows us to "receive a fulness of joy" (D&C 93:33).

There is a joy that comes from receiving a mortal body and then a greater joy that comes from receiving a celestial, resurrected body. We had to come to earth to receive a mortal body in order to eventually enjoy the types of bodies our Heavenly Parents have. Having a body also allows us to have the kind of mortal experience we need to have in order to develop the character and attributes of Heavenly Father.

WHAT ARE SOME WORDS YOU WOULD USE TO DESCRIBE HEAVENLY FATHER?

_____

_____

_____

_____

_____

WHAT WORDS DESCRIBE HIS PERSONALITY AND CHARACTER?

_____

_____

_____

_____

_____

In addition to not yet having a family or a resurrected body like Heavenly Father, we were different from Him in our CHARACTER. His character includes things like His kindness, His mercy, His understanding, His love, His patience, His justice, and His wisdom. The only way to acquire these attributes is to come to earth and have a mortal experience. We learn them through adversity, agency, relationships, experiences, and all of the aspects of life that come from a fallen world like the one we live in. We had to come to earth to learn these lessons. We had to leave the comfort of a heavenly home in order to grow and become like God. We could only develop these attributes in this kind of situation.

WAYS WE WERE DIFFERENT FROM AND CAN BECOME LIKE OUR HEAVENLY PARENTS

Family
Body
Character and Attributes

Each of us here on earth chose to follow our Heavenly Father's plan and come here for this mortal experience. WE HAD THE CHOICE. That was an important part of God's plan for us. He did not want to force us to become like Him. He did not want to force us to live in His presence forever. He wanted to give us the dignity of choosing that for ourselves. We needed to come to a place away from our heavenly home where we could decide if we wanted to follow Him and return to His presence. God wanted us to have the opportunity to choose Him.

However, even though it was necessary for us to choose for ourselves, our Father was not going to be neutral on the issue. He would not force our choice, but He would seek to win our hearts in ways that only He can—through loving relationships, the words and promises of the scriptures and prophets, the whisperings of the Holy Ghost, the peaceful feelings inside us when we hear truth, beautiful sunsets, the words to a song that hit us right in the heart, and other "coincidences" that are not by chance at all.

THE CHOICE IS OURS
TO LIVE WITH
AND LIVE LIKE HIM,
but our Father makes it clear
WHICH CHOICE HE WANTS
us to make.

Having the freedom to choose can be dangerous. As we will talk about in a later chapter, it means we have the chance to choose to ruin ourselves and hurt others. This world can be a scary place. It is important to know that God needed to send us away to become like Him and enjoy the life He has, but He would never have sent us away to a place of potential danger with a veil, agency, sickness, and trial without setting up a safety net.

THAT SAFETY NET IS
JESUS CHRIST.

The Father's plan could not have been possible without the atoning sacrifice of His Son. We have already talked about how sending Jesus Christ to the world was God's greatest way of showing us His love. Our ability to not only return to His presence but to become like Him is made possible only in and through the Savior. That is a part of why the gift of His Son is such a gift of love to us. The Father sent Jesus Christ to make His plan possible.

HE SENT JESUS TO GIVE US THE HOPE AND POSSIBILITY OF A GREATER POTENTIAL.

If we had stayed with Heavenly Father in the premortal heaven, we would have been happy and enjoyed our lives, but we would not have been able to have the fullness of joy that comes from experiencing mortality and becoming like Him. There are days when life in this world is so hard, but we could never become what we wanted to be and what our Heavenly Parents wanted us to be without coming here.

*Simply stated, the Father's plan is for us to become **like Him** and enjoy the life He has.*

The book of Job uses my favorite phrase about the premortal life when it says the "morning stars SANG TOGETHER, and all the sons of God SHOUTED FOR JOY" (Job 38:7) when they heard the plan. Truly, God's plan for us is one of the greatest ways He shows His love.

One summer, our family took a trip to California to visit some of the national parks there. One of the claims to fame for California is their forests of redwood and sequoia trees. These are massive, massive plants. Some of these trees can grow as tall as thirty stories high. To give you an idea of that scale, if you live in a two-story house, you would have to stack fifteen of them on top of each other to reach that height. These trees are giants!

As you take the roads through the park, you can drive right through the center of some trees through carved-out sections of the trunk. The largest sequoia tree in the world is in Sequoia National Park and is named "General Sherman." You know a tree is big if it has a name! "The General" is close to thirty stories high and weighs 2.7 million pounds. That is about the weight of nine blue whales. Nine! Some of the sequoia trees are the largest living single organisms on the earth.

One of the most mind-blowing things about these trees is the seeds that they come from. They are tiny! A sequoia or redwood seed is about the size and weight of a piece of dry oatmeal. If you were holding one and blinked too much, it might create enough wind to blow it out of your hand. I don't know if someone can really blink that fast, but you get the idea! They are so small.

These massive, impressive, giant trees all start out as the tiniest, seemingly insignificant little seeds. It takes them years and years to reach their full height, but it is incredible that the potential to become these towering skyscrapers is all inside these tiny little seeds. What would you miss if you tried to study sequoia or redwood trees by only studying the seeds? What would you not know about the trees if you only looked closely at their beginning, baby state?

The same is true of all of us. We are the seed form of our Heavenly Parents.

"As God now is, MAN MAY BECOME."[5]

We have the potential to grow and to become like Them—boys like their Heavenly Father and girls like their Heavenly Mother.[6] We can become like God in receiving the type of body He has, developing His attributes, and one day living in a marriage and family like Them. We likely recognized these ways of life that our Heavenly Parents enjoyed in the premortal world and longed to have them for ourselves. Heavenly Father created a plan for that to be possible.

I watched a video posted on Twitter of a sixteen-year-old boy gathered together with his family and friends to open his letter of acceptance to or rejection from Yale University. This is an experience that many of you will have soon as you prepare to leave home for college. Everyone was huddled around the computer as the young man opened his email containing the decision. When he clicked on it and everyone saw the word "accepted," the room erupted into applause. You would have thought the kid had won the Super Bowl. They were JUMPING and SHOUTING and SCREAMING and CRYING and HUGGING and DANCING. Everyone was. The kid who was about to leave. The mom and dad who would send him. All of his brothers, sisters, cousins, and friends, who knew what kind of experience this was going to be. They all cheered wildly! Would going to Yale be hard? Absolutely. There would be tests, failures, disappointments, late nights, late assignments, demanding professors, and empty bank accounts. But there would be friends made, lessons learned, beautiful experiences, so much fun, new points of view, and a refined soul. The boy's parents understood this better than him, and that is probably why they cheered the loudest.

I imagine this is what it was like when we left the presence of our heavenly home to come to earth. I like to picture our Heavenly Parents, our friends, and our brothers and sisters all gathered around as we began our journey. I like to think there were cheers and shouts and dancing and celebrations as we approached our time to come to the world.

Yes, it would be hard.
Yes, it would have its challenges. But the
EXPERIENCES we were about to have, the LESSONS
we would learn, and the way we would grow into the
people God intended for us to be would make it worth
it. This is a BEAUTIFUL LIFE, and the Father has a
beautiful plan. Everything He has arranged
on this EARTH is for us to reach our
ETERNAL POTENTIAL.

Each week, the young women of the Church rehearse this truth when they stand and say the Young Women Theme. In the list of values that they recite, one of them is "Divine Nature." That value is a reminder of our potential to become like Heavenly Father and Heavenly Mother.

It is a REMINDER of God's plan
for us as His children—the plan to be
a part of SOMETHING MAGNIFICENT.

Our Father did not drop us off at a park somewhere and wish us good luck in getting back home. He designed a plan to give us an experience we wanted. ONE THAT WE CHOSE. ONE THAT WAS WORTH FIGHTING FOR. We do not have all the details, and we know that we are still in seed form, but our Heavenly Father has not only made it possible but is working all day and all night to bring it about. IT IS HIS WORK AND HIS GLORY. His greatest happiness is to have His children happy. That is His plan. And it is a plan worth shouting for!

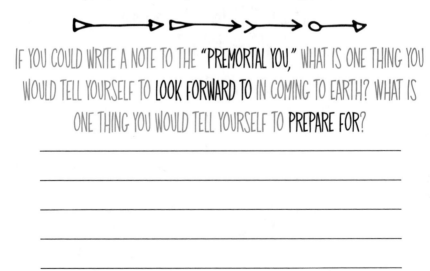

IF YOU COULD WRITE A NOTE TO THE "PREMORTAL YOU," WHAT IS ONE THING YOU WOULD TELL YOURSELF TO LOOK FORWARD TO IN COMING TO EARTH? WHAT IS ONE THING YOU WOULD TELL YOURSELF TO PREPARE FOR?

_____

_____

_____

_____

_____

ORANGES AND OTHER THINGS
GOD SHOWED LOVE BY CREATING THE WORLD

When Korihor, an anti-Christ in the Book of Mormon, came attacking Alma's beliefs, he demanded that Alma prove to him that there was a God. In a very clever defense, Alma turned the tables back on him.

"What evidence have ye that there is no God, or that Christ cometh not?" (Alma 30:40).

"You prove there *isn't* a God," he essentially said. "Why do I have to prove there is one?" Alma moved the burden of proof onto Korihor. The burden of proof is the responsibility to prove something right or wrong. Alma may have been wondering why the believer has to prove the existence of God. Why shouldn't the nonbeliever have to prove that God doesn't exist? Then Alma turned to the Creation.

"ALL THINGS DENOTE THERE IS A GOD; yea, even the earth, and all things that are upon the face of it, yea, and its motion, yea, and also all the planets which move in their regular form do witness that there is a SUPREME CREATOR" (Alma 30:44).

Alma was basically saying to Korihor, "If you want to say there is no God, then you need to come up with an explanation for everything that I see.

↓ ↓ ↓ ↓ ↓ ↓

ALL OF CREATION WITNESSES OF THE CREATOR.

You say there is no God? Well everything around me disagrees with you."

Think about the world around you. Look around at everything that was here waiting for you when you were born. There are a lot of theories about how the world came into existence. Even though we do not know the details of the Creation, we know that the Creation was not an accident.

IT WAS AN ACT OF LOVE. ♡

"We will go down, for there is space there, and we will take of these materials, and we will make an earth whereon these [our children] may dwell" (Abraham 3:24). Under the direction of the Father, Jesus Christ created the earth as a place for God's children to live and enjoy the experience He wanted them to have. Our Father sent us away from home, but He sent us to a place that He created and prepared for us.

A beautiful place! An amazing

♥ home away from home!

Think of the oceans. I have always been a lover of the ocean. One February I planned a spontaneous weekend trip to California when I found out that one of my friends had never been to the beach. That was not acceptable to me. People need to see the sea. And when I went, I packed the car full of friends and sunflower seeds and drove eleven hours there and back, all for a ten-minute swim in freezing cold waters simply because I love the ocean *that* much. Somehow two hydrogens and one oxygen have come together to create the lifeblood of this planet. Some scientists estimate that there are 326 million trillion gallons of water in the oceans.[7] How many zeroes is that?! No new water ever comes to the earth; it just cycles from the oceans to the clouds to the rain to the rivers and back to the oceans. All of it happening without any human assistance.

And what about trees? Think of all the trees and grasses and shrubbery. Magnificent! Think of it! An entire forest lives all packaged up in tiny seeds—waiting to be unleashed—one leaf at a time. And the flowers! So many types of flowers. Roses, sunflowers, daisies, irises, petunias, peonies, and lilies.

God planted them all so that life here could be more colorful and beautiful. Flowers for hanging pots on the front porch. Flowers for Austrian mountaintops. Flowers for weddings. Flowers for "I'm sorry." Flowers for "I love you." And flowers made specifically for wishing.

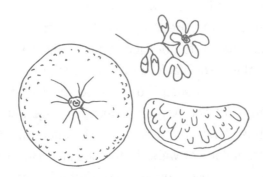

Some of those flowers even turn into fruit! Every time I see an orange I am convinced there is a God. How does a seed become a sapling, then become a plant, then become a tree that knows how to shoot out branches, leaves, and make food? First the branches grow flowers that turn into little green fruits that then change color to match their name, "orange," and then just drop from the branches when they are ready to be eaten. All packaged up and ready to go! And when you peel open the skin, you find that God already cut up the orange into little slices for you. Incredible!

For six days, God orchestrated and oversaw the creation of a place that would continually witness of His EXiSTENCE and His love. A day for light and dark. A day for water. A day for stars. A day for plants. A day for animals.

Think of it all! There was a day for everything!

VOLCANOES,	THE COLOR MAGENTA,
WIND,	SAND DUNES,
CLOWNFISH,	CLOUDS,
HIPPOS,	MT. KILIMANJARO,
LEMONS,	SEASHELLS,
CANYONS,	TRICERATOPS,
SUNSETS,	CHOCOLATE,
EMERALDS,	AND PUPPIES.

How could a God who created chocolate and puppies not love us?

My science teacher often called Earth the Goldilocks planet. Not too hot and not too cold. It is in the precise spot in the solar system for life to exist like it does. Not too close and not too far from that beastly, burning ball of gas we call the sun. Amazing.

And for a moment, let's consider the sun and sky. If the world around you has not caused enough excitement, it is time to look to the heavens.

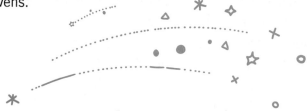

The stars are endless. THEY SURELY WITNESS OF GOD. Have you ever gazed at the stars longer than five minutes without wondering—without slipping into amazement? There have been times when I have been far enough away from the city lights that I have been able to see just how many stars there are. It is electrifying to see the whole night sky filled with twinkling lights. And then God has them shoot across the horizon just to thrill your soul. (Another chance to make a wish!)

And then when you visit a planetarium you learn that the stars you can see—the ones that you cannot even count—are not even the tip of the iceberg.

Moses once turned to the sky and said, "Behold, the heaven and the heaven of heavens is the Lord's thy God, *the earth also,* with all that therein is" (Deuteronomy 10:14; emphasis added).

Do you love that the earth—the 197 million square miles of earth[8]—is an afterthought in that verse? " . . . the earth also . . ."

It is because not only the heavens, but the heaven of heavens— wherever that is—belongs to God. He created and oversees all of it. All 100 billion stars of our baby Milky Way Galaxy and the countless galaxies out in endless space that are expanding in every direction every minute of the day. ALL Of iT.

Some astronomers believe that the number of stars in the known universe is more than the number of grains of sand on all the beaches of the earth.[9] Imagine taking a walk on the beach, stop- ping, kneeling down, licking your thumb, and pressing it into the sand. How many grains of sand do you think would stick to your wet thumb? Now imagine looking down the whole beach you are on. And then multiplying that by every beach on the earth. That is a lot of grains of sand. That is a lot of stars. A lot of suns!

READY TO RELISH IN GOD'S CREATIONS FOR A MINUTE?

Favorite fruit? _____

Favorite flower? _____

Coolest place you've ever been?

_____

Bucket list vacation spot?

_____

Ever seen a shooting star? Yes ☐   No ☐

An animal that fascinates you?

_____

An animal you want as a pet?

_____

Sunsets or sunrises? (Circle one)

Mountain or beach? (Circle one)

HOW DID THESE ALL GET HERE?
HOW WERE THEY MADE?

We don't know **HOW**, but we do know **WHY**.

God said to Moses, who must have had an interest in stars, "The heavens, they are many, and they cannot be numbered unto man; BUT THEY ARE NUMBERED UNTO ME, FOR THEY ARE MINE" (Moses 1:37). Our language does not have a number that is big enough to describe the number of God's creations, but He wanted to be sure that Moses knew that they were numbered to Him. He knows every one of His creations. They were created on purpose. And why did He create it all? For us.

Every WAVE, every SPARROW, every DANDELION was created for us.

The world is a gift. A detailed and deliberate gift of love.

Just one creation is enough evidence of God's love, and there is so much more than one. Much more than we could ever count. His love is witnessed in His creations all around us. EVERYWHERE. EVERY DAY. If I were Alma, and Korihor came attacking me about the love and existence of God, there is a lot I could point out to him to prove my belief, but I think I would just take him to the beach—or toss him an orange.

THE CROWNING CREATION
GOD SHOWS US LOVE BY GIVING US OUR BODIES

One year I tried an experiment at church. I went into a Young Women class and asked all of the young women what God's greatest creation was. I got lots of different answers. Mountains, dolphins, sunsets, butterflies. All good ones. I then walked down the hall into the room where the priests quorum was meeting. I poked my head in and asked the same question.

"Boys, what is God's greatest creation?"

Almost in unison, the class responded, "Girls!"

On this matter, and perhaps only on this matter, the boys were right and the girls were wrong.

The list of God's creations is quite impressive. There is a lot in this world to hear, see, taste, and experience, as we saw in our last chapter. But after the water, the land, the light, the stars, the plants, and the animals came God's crowning creation: people.[10]

Even though we use the word *creation* with people, we are not merely His creations—we are His children.

WE ARE NOT ART PROJECTS
OR HOBBIES.
WE ARE HIS **LITERAL** OFFSPRING.

As the Family Proclamation says, "All human beings—male and female—are created in the image of God." THIS MEANS THAT WE ALL LOOK LIKE OUR HEAVENLY PARENTS. Men look like their Father in Heaven and women are created in the image of their Mother in Heaven. We have eyes to see because they have eyes to see. We have hands to hold because they have hands to hold. We look alike and we have the potential to become like Them in all ways.

When our Heavenly Father sent us to earth, He gave us our bodies as a gift of His love.

We are **spiritual** beings who
are having a **mortal** experience,

and we get to experience mortality in these amazing bodies. One day, we will all live forever in resurrected bodies like our Heavenly Father does. Those bodies will be perfect, whole, and complete. The bodies we received at birth will be the very bodies that will be resurrected. THE GIFT OF OUR BODIES IS AN ETERNAL GIFT.

During our time here on earth, our bodies are mortal. That means they can feel pain and sickness. They can get tired or worn out at the end of a day.

Our bodies get more tired and more worn out toward the end of a life. Our bodies are also tempted by things of the world—things like laziness and lust. One day, all of our bodies will die. ALL OF THESE ASPECTS OF OUR BODY ARE FOR A GREAT PURPOSE IN GOD'S PLAN. Throughout our life we can choose to overcome and have self-mastery over the imperfections and temptations of our bodies. Overcoming those things makes our spirits stronger and more like the character of God.

In addition to our bodies providing us a necessary growing opportunity, our bodies were also given to us as a GIFT OF ENJOYMENT. God sent us to such a beautiful and wonderful world to live our lives and experience His plan, and these bodies are made to help us enjoy it!

OUR BODIES ARE AMAZING.

We have eyes that have lenses that outdo any camera you could dream of. How many pixels are they? And how many colors can they comprehend? Whatever Apple or Samsung comes up with next, it will be a distant second place to the cameras that God gave us built-in. We see sunsets with them, watch movies, look at fireworks, read Harry Potter, and recognize friends and family.

Our ears catch vibrations in the air that are interpreted into sounds of every kind. What is the difference between laughter sound waves, cow moo sound waves, and Korean pop music sound waves? I have no clue. But our ears figure it out. They capture the music of the world.

WHAT iS yOUR FAVORiTE SOUND?

_____

We have feet that walk, skip, jump, lunge, run, leap, and dance. We have lungs that breathe in the oxygen all around us—the oxygen that trees somehow produce and spit out into the air—those trees again! And what about our magnificent hearts? Your heart beats more than 100,000 times per day without you having to do anything. It pumps over 2,000 gallons of blood per day to every part of your body—to your seeing eyes, your hearing ears, and those dancing feet.

That heart beats day in and day out without you even thinking about it. But the beauty is, if you want to, you *can* think about it. Because you can think! God gave you a mind. And you can dream and remember and imagine. I have always thought that the fact that you and I can reason and argue about the existence of God proves that there is a God.

 The ability for a **mind** to comprehend and seek and wonder **is a wonder** in and of itself!

Perhaps the greatest aspect of our bodies is that our Father has put into us the ability to be a part of the creation process with Him. Our bodies are able to create and bear children of our own. This is an experience that God wanted us to have as one of the most beautiful aspects of life on earth. Elder David A. Bednar taught, "The most sacred of all our divine powers is to become a co-creator with Heavenly Father in providing physical bodies for His spirit sons and daughters and in establishing a righteous and Christ-centered family. Nothing is more holy; nothing deserves more reverence; nothing is more central to the plan of happiness."[11]

OUR BODIES TRULY ARE A BEAUTIFUL GIFT, AND THEY ARE AWESOME!

Speaking of that, have you ever seen the "people are awesome" videos on YouTube? I watch those with my eyes and jaw wide open. I saw one the other day of a giant seesaw set up on a beach. A guy jumped onto one side of the seesaw and launched the guy on the other side up into the air, where he did a double backflip. Then that guy landed on his side of the seesaw, launching the first guy up to do his own double backflip. They went back and forth, launching each other into double backflips. It was incredible!

People truly are amazing. Think of it!

People discover masterpieces hidden in marble chunks,
construct towers that scrape the sky,
tickle ivories in the right order to create stirring melodies,
improvise rap battles, land double kickflips,
launch Kickstarters, start and finish Ironmans,
touch the top of Mt. Everest and the floor of the Dead Sea,
write poetry, fly rockets,
pitch no-hitters, dance hip-hop,
learn French, surf waves,
perform open-heart surgery,
bake crème brûlée, fiddle, juggle, clog,
and have invented the Reese's Peanut Butter Cup.

The list is endless, and will keep getting more impressive, because we are the CHILDREN OF AN ENDLESSLY IMPRESSIVE GOD. He is the one who paints the sky at each sunset and taps out the rhythm of the tides. He is the great CREATOR and MASTER ARCHITECT of the entire universe. All of our gifts—physical and spiritual—are gifts from Him.

List five of your **favorite people** and **one thing** that each does amazingly **well.**

1.	
2.	
3.	
4.	
5.	

All of our bodies are different. The variety of bodies and people in this world adds to the majesty of it. We have different sizes, shapes, races, and abilities. That gives so much beauty and variety. We wouldn't want it any other way! Some are born to this earth with limited physical or mental abilities. President Russell M. Nelson, who had a successful career as a heart surgeon, once taught that we should be "reminded that a perfect body is not required to achieve one's divine destiny. In fact, some of the sweetest spirits are housed in frail or imperfect bodies. GREAT SPIRITUAL STRENGTH IS OFTEN DEVELOPED BY PEOPLE WITH PHYSICAL CHALLENGES, precisely because they are so challenged."[12] Any physical limitations in this world are only temporary, and

GOD WILL USE THOSE TEMPORARY SITUATIONS TO CREATE ETERNAL BEAUTY.

There are some who live with sadness because they compare themselves, their abilities, and their bodies to other people. There are others who treat their bodies with disrespect. This happens when we forget that our bodies were a gift—a gift that was given to show us how much God loves us. WE DID NOT EARN OUR BODIES; THEY WERE GIVEN TO US FREELY, AND THEY WILL BE OURS TO KEEP IN AN EVENTUAL PERFECTED STATE THANKS TO THE GREAT COST THAT CHRIST PAID.

Because our Father loves us, we get to experience this amazing world in these amazing bodies. Then, one day, they will be perfected and glorified and united with our spirits eternally. I saw a T-shirt once that said, "I know I'm somebody 'cause God don't make no junk." Amen! He sure doesn't. That truth comes to us on T-shirts AND in the scriptures. After every day of the Creation, the scriptures say that "God saw it and it was good." Then after the last day, when man and woman, His crowning work, were on the earth, the book of Genesis says that God said "it was *very* good" (Genesis 1:31; emphasis added).

I KNOW I'M SOMEBODY 'CAUSE GOD DON'T MAKE NO JUNK.

The "VERY GOOD" Creator of these "VERY GOOD" BODIES not only numbered the stars in the heaven but has numbered the hairs on our head (see Luke 12:7). He watches over and sees us with His caring eyes and hears our prayers with His attentive ears. One day, we will return to His presence, and in our bodies, we will embrace Him once again and He will hold us close and tight in His loving arms.[13]

And if I haven't learned yet by then, I want Him to teach me how to do a double backflip.

SUNDAY NIGHTS
GOD SHOWS US LOVE BY GIVING US FAMILIES

Every Sunday evening, Jenny, the kids, and I jump into our big black bus and drive to my aunt Suz and uncle Jeff's house for dinner. I have been going to their house for Sunday dinner ever since my freshman year of college. Everyone is always invited to the Bunkers', and Suz and Jeff would welcome you with open arms before they even learned your name. You should come sometime!

You might want to come on the Sunday before Christmas for the annual fondue night and wildly rambunctious white elephant game. We look forward to it with as much anticipation as we do Christmas morning. You can dip anything in chocolate. Or maybe you want to come for Halloween cookie night. That one is a winner! You will find sprinkles in your clothes and hair for a good three weeks afterwards. The Easter egg hunt has evolved into the most epic event of the year. It has escalated from eggs being nicely hidden under couch cushions to eggs under the floorboards of the trunk of the car, tied to balloons floating 100 yards above the house, or buried six inches underground in the middle of the backyard. One year, we sent an egg to Italy and the only clue we gave to find it was in Latin—*Eritque arcus gustare.*

You could actually come on any Sunday and you would love it just the same. You could sit on the patio with us and argue about pop culture, build puzzles with Caleb in the living room, or sit at the dining room table with Aunt Laura and walk away after your conversation feeling smarter and like a million bucks. She has that gift. We laugh together, we scoop ice cream together, we fight over the dinner rolls, we celebrate each other's successes, and we give advice when someone brings a problem to the table. We have stood together in baby blessing circles, danced together at a long-awaited wedding, cheered loudly together at mission call openings, and cried together in the living room that has now become one of my favorite spots on earth.

I know not every family or family dinner looks like this one, but I am sharing the positive aspects we can all hope for, contribute toward, and plan on creating someday. We all have different families and family situations. Some are ideal, some may seem ideal from the outside, and others couldn't feel further from the ideal. My family is as messy and imperfect a group of people as you can find anywhere else in the world, but before we eat dinner each Sunday, my youngest cousin, Adam, chooses someone to pray, and

we all bow our heads
and thank God
for the food and
for our family.

God is CREATIVE and POWERFUL, and there are a million ways He could have chosen to send us to earth. The way He decided to do it was by sending us into families. His hope was to have all of His children sent to a mom and a dad who would raise them in a family who would love them, care for them, and stand with them through their journey on this earth. I once heard someone say that God couldn't be everywhere at once, and that is why He gave us mothers. I would change that quote and expand it a little more to say, "THAT IS WHY HE GAVE US FAMILIES."

Heavenly Father never intended for us to experience life on earth by ourselves. Because He loves us so much, He sent us to families to be with us while we were here. After Adam was placed in the Garden of Eden, God said,

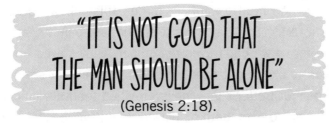

"IT IS NOT GOOD THAT THE MAN SHOULD BE ALONE"
(Genesis 2:18).

That statement is true for all of us. To solve that problem for Adam, God created Eve and then gave them the power to make a family.

God has commanded husbands and wives, parents and families to raise their children and look out for each other in love and righteousness. This doesn't always happen, but it has always been the hope and ideal. Families look very different from each other, and there are varied circumstances we all grow up in. In any of these situations there can still be love, care, and righteousness.

No matter what your family situation looks like, GOD iS WATCHiNG OVER YOU, SENDING HiS LOVE, AND PLANNiNG A BEAUTiFUL FUTURE FOR YOU. Some of us get to enjoy a part of the ideal now, and everyone has the opportunity to create the home he or she would like in the future.

What is one thing you love about your family now?

_____

What is one thing you want for your family in the future?

_____

A popular Primary song teaches us that "God gave us families to help us become what He wants us to be—this is how He shares His love, for THE FAMiLY iS OF GOD."[14] Most of what our parents, and others, have done for us we don't even remember. They stayed up all night rocking you to sleep, put together cribs, buckled car seats, cut the crust off peanut butter sandwiches, brushed teeth, practiced spelling words, helped with math homework, paid for checkups, went on zoo trips, bought soccer cleats, replaced shoes you lost and socks you kept wearing outside, put together the swing set, taught you to ride a two-wheeler, took you to baseball practice, bought ridiculously expensive dance costumes you only wore once, and paid for piano lessons you hated. And—wait!—I didn't even mention diapers and potty training. That should have gone first. As thankful as we are for these things and so many more, they are not even the greatest gifts we receive from our parents. They teach us how to love, how to sacrifice, how to work, and how to believe. GOD TEACHES US OUR MOST VALUABLE LESSONS THROUGH OUR PARENTS. iN FACT, iT iS USUALLY THROUGH OUR PARENTS THAT WE LEARN ABOUT GOD.

Will you write a THANK-YOU LETTER here to your parents or other loved ones for all they have done for you? You might take a picture of it and send it to them or copy it and send it in a text. Or, better yet, tell them in person.

We learn and gain so much from our parents. This can also be true for brothers and sisters and other family members. There are HABITS, STRENGTHS, and UNDERSTANDING that we all learn from each other. My dad has taught me tenderness. My mom has given me the gift of radical giving. My sister Christy has taught me to be fiercely loyal. John has taught me how to serve. Jacquelyn has shown me how to love. Lindsey has modeled courage and sweetness. And Britt has shown me how to have determination. Growing up all together has helped me to see my parents' and siblings' gifts and traits and has given me a desire to seek them in my own journey. And where I have fallen very, very short, someone else in my family has been able to make up the difference.

In families, God has given us defenders, teammates, cheerleaders, problem solvers, hope givers, and truth tellers. I know I always have someone on my side, someone to think about and pray for me, someone to ask about me, and someone who fights for me. We can feel God's strength through our families.

List the members of your family and one thing each of them has taught you.

I remember a time I was lying in a hospital bed and was a little bit upset with God. I wondered why He wasn't intervening or helping. If He understood how I felt, then where was He? Why hadn't He shown up?

In the middle of one of those nights, I woke up suddenly from a deep sleep. I looked over and saw my mom asleep in a chair next to my hospital bed. She was half covered by a thin hospital blanket and propped up in the most uncomfortable sleeping position she could've been in. In that moment, God whispered to me, "I AM HERE. I SENT YOUR MOM." We not only learn from each other, but we are there for each other.

Families not only fight for each other, but sometimes (maybe often) they fight with each other. God knew that we would not all get along all the time.

HE KNEW WE WOULD DISAGREE, BE SELFISH, ANNOY EACH OTHER, AND TEST EACH OTHER'S PATIENCE. YET, HE STILL SENT US HERE INTO FAMILIES.

Families take work and sacrifice and compromise. Sometimes living alone seems easier, but there are lessons we learn together that simply could not be learned on our own. We become more refined and our rough places get smoothed out by rubbing against each other. When someone doesn't replace the toilet paper, or steals the shotgun seat in the car, or learns which of your buttons to push and then pushes them over and over, or gets the better present at Christmas, or wrestles you to the floor when your parents aren't home (or any of the other acts of barbarianism that happen when parents aren't home), we learn lessons and grow in a way we could not grow by ourselves.

This is an official and public apology to Lindsey for tying her to the garage door.

Dad's jokes are rarely good, Mom isn't always the most rational human, our siblings can bug, and family reunions might not be the most exciting things on the planet, but A LOT OF GOOD IS HAPPENING UNDERNEATH IT ALL. The attributes of patience, love, and long-suffering are virtues that God hopes for us to learn. In the long run, they make us happier. We learn from both the gifts and weaknesses of each other. The situation is set up perfectly for us to become what He wants us to BECOME.

Some of you reading this chapter may feel sad about the family situation you have. Everyone has agency, and sometimes that means that families suffer because of other people's choices.

There is **no perfect** family in the world—no matter what they **might look like** at church!

But there are definitely some family situations that are far from ideal and some that are even downright hurtful. Broken relationships, abandonment, abuse, and other severe problems plague many families. Some situations are heartbreaking, some just annoying, and some are not the ideal pattern that the Lord may have intended for families.

There are a few things to remember that might be helpful when our reality falls short of the ideal. First, no matter what someone's family looks like, GOD IS THERE. He is a perfect Father. You are never without parents who care and love you deeply. Because of the love that He has, HE WILL COMPENSATE FOR THE THINGS THAT ARE LACKING IN YOUR LIFE. Often, He will send other people into your life who can fill in where others may be missing. If you are in a family situation that you wish were different, my advice would be to try your best to be the best family member that you can (as long as it is not an abusive situation—in those cases you should always talk to someone for some help). BE PATIENT. BE LOVING. BE HELPFUL. BE THANKFUL. You are still learning wonderful lessons and growing into a person more like your Heavenly Parents. So keep at it the best you can. You might not solve all of the problems, and you may feel like nothing changes no matter how hard you try. Sometimes this happens. It isn't your fault, and God is so happy with your efforts. You did not get to pick your family situation, but one day, you *will* get to choose who you want to marry and the kind of home that you want to raise your own kids in. In the meantime, DO YOUR **VERY BEST** AND KEEP ASKING GOD TO TEACH YOU THE LESSONS **YOU CAN LEARN** FROM YOUR FAMILY.

Is there **one habit** or **practice** you could try out this week to improve your life at home? Something **small**. Something **simple**. Will you do it? You might be surprised by the impact you can have at home.

This week I will . . .

_____

_____

_____

One year, after a Christmas dinner at my grandparents' house—after all the presents had been opened and our bellies hurt from too much laughter and cherry pie—my grandpa, Pom Pom, stood up and got everyone's attention. He is soft spoken and not very tall, but the sweetness in his heart could fill an entire football stadium. He asked us to look around at everyone who was there and to think about those who were not. He told us that THiS WAS OUR FAMiLY. We are a mess, and we aren't perfect, but this is the family we were sent to. And then, in a way that only Pom Pom could, he made a plea.

"Take care of each other," he said.
"Always look out for each other. That is what families do."

I like to believe that a very similar conversation happened with our Heavenly Parents before we came to earth—that They wrapped us all up in Their love and told us to look around at each other. And then I think They had the same request.

"Take care of each other."

We are all here as one big family. THE FAMILY OF GOD. We have our own parents, siblings, cousins, and people that we spend family reunions with, but we are all brothers and sisters. I have friends and neighbors that I consider as much a part of my family as I do my own blood. They are my tribe. My people. Our true family is much bigger than the one we spend Christmas morning with. WE ARE ALL HERE TO TAKE CARE OF EACH OTHER. TO LEARN FROM EACH OTHER. TO LOVE EACH OTHER. God sent us all here at the same time. The kid down the street, the girl who works at Chick-fil-A, the boy in your math class, the quarterback from the other team. We are all in this together. Our Father in Heaven designed it like this because of how much He loves us.

HE COULDN'T BE DOWN HERE WITH US, SO HE GAVE US EACH OTHER.

So I say, we either all go back together, or none of us go back at all.

And when we get there, let's all gather for a Sunday night dinner. I'll hide your Easter egg.

{ YOU MIGHT WANT TO SEND A TEXT TO SOMEONE IN YOUR FAMILY OR WRITE A FAMILY GROUP TEXT TO SIMPLY ENCOURAGE THEM OR SAY YOU LOVE THEM. SEEMS LIKE A GOOD THING TO DO TODAY, DOESN'T IT? }

8

OPPOSITES

GOD SHOWS US LOVE BY ALLOWING SIN AND ADVERSITY

Last summer, I was in Germany and had the chance to visit the Dachau Concentration Camp outside of Munich. Dachau was used as a place to illegally imprison and persecute Jews and other groups of people during World War II. The crimes committed at concentration camps were horrible. The morning of our visit, before we left, I found a quiet place to pray before I hopped into the car. My prayer was simple.

"HEAVENLY FATHER, JUST LET ME KNOW THAT YOU WERE THERE WHEN IT HAPPENED. PLEASE LET ME KNOW THEY WERE NOT ALONE."

In high school, I had the best history teacher in the world. He helped us learn the stories of the past with compassion and empathy and in the most memorable ways. He spent a lot of time on World War II and the terrible things that happened in concentration camps. I remember being deeply impacted during his presentation on the Holocaust. I could not understand why God would let it happen. It didn't make any sense to me. As the years went by, I didn't think about it every day, but whenever the subject came up in a movie or something I saw online, it brought back those same confused and hurt feelings. I have learned a few things since high school, and I knew God was a loving God even though these things had happened, but I wanted to feel in my heart during my visit that He had been present.

It was overcast and rainy the morning we went to Dachau, which seemed to fit the mood of the place. We walked through crowded bunk rooms, places of punishment and torture, gas chambers, and oven rooms. It was depressing to see, and yet, as we walked through

I FELT PEACE.

I felt part of the sadness our Heavenly Father had for the horrible things that had happened there. I also felt an assurance that

HE HAD NEVER LEFT THEM.

Two months later, I spoke at a devotional at a college campus. I had planned on sharing a little about this story and the feelings and testimony I received while I was there. Before I spoke, there was a choir musical number that I will never forget. It was a song based on a poem that is believed to have been written by a prisoner in a concentration camp in Germany. The prisoner, who is unknown, scratched the words into the wall of the cellar where he lived. These are some of the words from that poem:[15]

"I believe through any trial,
there is always a way
But sometimes in this suffering
and hopeless despair
My heart cries for shelter,
to know someone's there
But a voice rises within me, saying, hold on,
my child, I'll give you strength,
I'll give you hope.
Just stay a little while.

I believe in the sun
even when it is not shining
And I believe in love
even when there's no one there
But I believe in God
even when he is silent."

As the choir sang words inspired by the poem, my heart surged with a belief in the love of God despite the bad things that happen in this world. It was the kind of love that even reached a prisoner in the cellar of a concentration camp.

THAT IS POWERFUL LOVE.

There is a lot of pain, disappointment, and tragedy on this earth. Sometimes, people take that as evidence that God does not love us. I once had a conversation with someone who said there were three truths about God that seemed to contradict each other. These were the statements:

EVIL AND BAD EXIST.
GOD IS ALL-POWERFUL.
GOD IS ALL-LOVING.

His reasoning was that all three statements cannot be true at the same time. The first point is certain. There is definitely evil and heartache in this world. This can range anywhere from kidnapping to hurricanes to cancer. We will talk about different types of hardships later. But, for now, we know that the first point is certain. Evil and bad exist.

The second two are where the supposed contradiction is. If evil and bad exist, then God cannot be all-loving AND all-powerful. For example, imagine an earthquake kills hundreds of people in South America. If God were all-loving, then He would want to stop the earthquake from happening, right? So if the earthquake happened, He must not be all-powerful. He must not have been *able* to stop the earthquake. A loving person would obviously want to prevent it. So if He is all-powerful, and *CAN* stop the earthquake, then He must not be all-loving. If He could've stopped the earthquake but just sat and watched it happen, He must not truly love. Can you see the argument?

Many people may be confused by this and want to know which one is true. Is God all-loving or all-powerful? They know that evil and bad are in the world. They see it and experience it. They cannot figure out how a God who is all-loving *and* all-powerful allows these things to happen. So is God not powerful enough to stop it, or is He not loving enough to stop it?

The answer is neither.

GOD IS ALL-POWERFUL.
GOD IS ALL-LOVING.

Yes, evil and bad still exist, but that does not make the other statements false.

All three are true.

To understand how this is possible, we need to back up a little to the Garden of Eden. First, we need to remember the whole reason for and purpose of God's plan that we talked about a few chapters ago. It is so important to know that the reason He sent us here was to BECOME more like Him. Without knowing this, we could easily be confused by bad things happening to good people. Our experiences in this world were set up with our potential as the end goal—TO BE LIKE GOD.

When my son prays, he usually asks that we have a fun time. I think God is a joyful and fun Father, but His whole purpose for us is not only that we have a fun time. The world is not Disneyland, and His plan was not only about fun and comfort. The world is a school, and we came to grow and progress. The only way we could change and develop to become like Him was to live in a world of opposites.

When Adam and Eve ate the forbidden fruit in the Garden of Eden, the conditions of the world changed. This event is called the Fall. One of the effects of the Fall was opposition, or opposites. In the Garden of Eden, Adam and Eve did not have sickness, pain, tiredness, or hunger. They also did not have sadness, sin, death, or misery. Sounds great, huh? It was a paradise. However, they didn't *know* it was paradise.

If you don't have any of those "BAD" things, you also don't have any "GOOD."

For example, did Adam and Eve know that they were healthy if they had never gotten the flu? Could they appreciate health? Of course not. What about happiness? If there wasn't any sadness, then there couldn't be happiness. If there wasn't any sin, it means they couldn't be righteous. They did not have the choice to be good because there was no chance to be bad. Adam and Eve were just in neutral. They could not become like God. Here is how the prophet Lehi explained it to his kids:

"For it must needs be, that there is an OPPOSITION IN ALL THINGS. If not so, . . . righteousness could not be brought to pass, neither wickedness, neither holiness nor misery, neither good nor bad . . . , nor corruption nor incorruption, happiness nor misery, neither sense nor insensibility" (2 Nephi 2:11).

They were in neutral. In the Garden of Eden, Adam and Eve could never progress to become like their Heavenly Parents. They needed opposition—or opposites. When they ate the fruit, all of these opposites came into the world. Even though we do not like some of the negative experiences and choices, we would not get rid of them, because that would then get rid of ALL choices and experiences—including the good. It would ruin God's purposes and plan. HE WANTED US TO BECOME RIGHTEOUS AND GOOD AND HAPPY. That can only happen in a world where there is wickedness and bad and misery.

And so here we are. We live in a world that is fallen. It is a world that has

LIGHT AND DARK,
HEALTH AND SICKNESS,
GOOD AND BAD,
PLEASURE AND PAIN,
RIGHTEOUSNESS AND SIN.

These are the conditions that we need to choose righteousness, experience happiness, and grow to become more like God. These opposites are a gift of love to us. It's the only way.

So do we like the Fall? YES.

Do we like happiness? YES.

Do we like health? YES.

Do we like hatred? NO.

But if there was no hatred, there would be no kindness.

So, do we like hatred? NO, BUT YES.

We do not like when people choose it, but we would not get rid of the choice. That is true of all the opposites.

Because of this world of opposition, we will all experience heartache, sadness, and pain. (Don't forget that this means we experience happiness and joy, too!) There are a few different categories of adversity or hardships that we may experience in life:

Consequences of our own bad choices

NEGATIVE CONSEQUENCES OF OTHER PEOPLE'S CHOICES

Natural consequences of the Fall

Let's start with choices. A few Christmases ago, my friend pulled into her garage after a family party. When she got out of her car and shut the door, she turned and was face to face with a stranger. He had on dark clothes and held a gun to her chest, demanding she give him something or he would shoot. Luckily, she had cash in her pocket from a Christmas gift and it was enough to satisfy the criminal.

He ran off and she ran into her house, frightened and flustered. Why would God allow that man to terrorize women like that? Other people's stories are much worse, but the question is still the same. WHY DIDN'T GOD STOP IT FROM HAPPENING? He could've easily just thumped the bad guy on his way to the garage. If He loved my friend, why didn't He stop the criminal?

Have you ever wondered this before?

The privilege and gift and power to choose between good and evil is called agency. God will not force us to be righteous, love Him, return to Him, or become like Him. We must choose it for ourselves. Choosing God for ourselves is what helps us become more like Him. When you have a chance to do wrong and then decide to choose good, you become more like our good God. There have to be opposites and there has to be choice. If God stopped every bad choice from happening, then we really wouldn't have agency. And without agency, we would be in neutral again—not good or bad, happy or miserable, just neutral. SO BECAUSE HE LOVES US, GOD ALLOWS US TO CHOOSE. Most of the time, He doesn't stop bad choices from happening, even though He can. That would ruin the plan. It wouldn't be true agency if God prevented all bad choices.

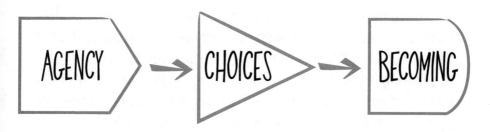

Preserving agency of course includes our own choices. IT WOULD NOT BE TRUE AGENCY IF GOD STOPPED US FROM MAKING WRONG CHOICES—even though those choices can cause negative consequences in our lives and the lives of others. If someone decides to drink and drive and gets into a car accident, that was not God's fault (even though sometimes God gets blamed for our bad choices). It was the fault of the person who decided to drink and drive. That decision will distance a person from God, cause personal heartache and guilt, and could be much worse depending on the damage that was caused. God lets this happen even if it hurts you or other innocent victims involved in the accident. We are going to talk about this more later, but it is important to mention here that even though God lets us choose and experience the consequence of our choices, HE ALSO PROVIDED THE CHANCE TO BE FORGIVEN, BE HEALED, AND MAKE THINGS RIGHT.

The reason you might have such a hard time with God not stopping bad things from happening is because you have such a good heart! It is a heart that is so much like His. If you are walking down the hallway at school and a girl in a wheelchair drops all of her books and papers, you would help her pick them up. If you have the power and opportunity to help someone, you do it, right?

If you didn't help her, you might be labeled as mean and insensitive. This is why God gets labeled mean and insensitive. He has the power and opportunity to stop all bad things. Because He doesn't, people assume it is because there is something wrong with His heart. But now you know why He usually doesn't. If He stopped every bad choice, then the whole plan would be ruined. No one would have the chance to be happy and become like Him.

It breaks God's heart when He sees the bad choices people make.

He cries when He sees His children hurting themselves and each other, but He loves us so much He lets it happen.

> The ability to choose
> is more important
> than the pain it causes
> when people choose badly.

Life was miserable for many of the Christians who lived after Jesus' Resurrection and Ascension into heaven. There was a lot of persecution against the people who believed and followed His teachings. Early in the book of Acts, we find a story that shows us how painful it is when God allows bad things to happen to good people. Two friends and Apostles, Peter and James, were in prison. Herod, the wicked king, knew that it pleased the people of Jerusalem to fight against the Christians. So he arrested these Apostles illegally, put them in jail, and announced an execution date for them. Could you imagine if that happened today?

What if you woke up tomorrow morning and heard the news that two of our Church leaders were in jail and scheduled to die. The whole Church would pray and fast and beg God to release them. That seems like a worthy and righteous request, doesn't it? CERTAINLY GOD WOULD INTERVENE. Then we read what happened in Acts 12.

"Now about that time Herod the king stretched forth his hands to vex certain of the church. And he killed James the brother of John with the sword" (Acts 12:1–2).

Just like that! Two verses in and the great Apostle James was killed. God allowed wicked people to execute him. You cannot help but wonder why. We have more questions as we keep reading. The night before Peter's execution, God sent an angel to the jail. Even though Peter was chained to two guards with fourteen others standing by and was kept in the deepest part of the prison, he was miraculously set free by the angel. While we are so happy this happened, again, we are left wondering why.

Why did James get the sword and Peter get the angel?

They were both good men and devoted and dedicated disciples. God intervened for one and not for the other.

A TIME I FELT LIKE I GOT THE SWORD:

A TIME I FELT LIKE I GOT THE ANGEL:

Sometimes this happens. Sometimes we get the sword and sometimes we get the angel, and we don't know why. But God does, and He has perfect, loving reasons for it. Peter and James were both worthy of miracles. WE ALL ARE WORTHY OF GOD'S MIRACLES. They come because we are His children. But He is God and He is our Father, and He knows what is best for each of us individually. He knows when to intervene and He knows when to let things happen. Sometimes we may think we know better when He should intervene, but really we just want our pain and suffering to be prevented. He has created countless universes. WE SHOULD TRUST HIM, EVEN WHEN IT IS HARD.

One day I was at Especially for Youth sharing these scriptures with one of the classes. A boy raised his hand to make a comment. He told us that sometimes the sword turns into an angel. When I asked what he meant, he told us that he almost did not come to EFY that year because his father had recently died in a car accident. Their family got the sword. But he also said he felt like God sent the angel, too. Their family had learned compassion, been blessed by little miracles, and had become closer to each other and God through that experience than they ever had before. He said he did not think that God caused the car accident, but he knew that God allowed it.

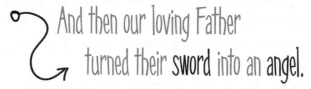

And then our loving Father turned their sword into an angel.

He has the ability and power to do that. When this young man was done sharing one of the most beautiful testimonies I had ever heard, I asked him his name.

"It's Peter," he said.

"Of course it is," I said back.

A LESSON I LEARNED THROUGH A TIME I GOT THE **SWORD**:

_____

_____

_____

_____

The effects of the Fall bring natural adversity as well. This means there will be accidents and people will die young or get sick or have birth defects. It also means there are natural disasters—earthquakes, tsunamis, and floods. Only a world filled with opposition can help us to become stronger. Every athlete knows this lesson. We only get faster and stronger when we work against weight. If God healed or prevented every sickness and stopped every natural disaster, it would not be a world of opposites. HE ALLOWS THESE THINGS TO HAPPEN SO THAT HIS PLAN CAN MOVE FORWARD. He sits with crying parents when they bury their young children and mourns when a family has lost everything in a flood, but if He stopped those things, He would stop everyone's chance to become like Him and enjoy ultimate happiness.

Like my friend Peter, I do not think God causes the pain and tragedies of this world to happen, but He does allow them, BECAUSE OF LOVE. He loves us enough to keep opposition. He loves us enough to allow agency. Even though the conditions of this world are part of His plan, God would never send His children to a world like this without His help.

Every SWORD
we receive in this world
can be turned into an ANGEL
if we TURN TO GOD.

God can HEAL us when we are
hurt, disappointed, or lonely.

He can FORGIVE us when we make mistakes
and sin against ourselves and others.

All of THE UNFAIR THINGS about our lives
WILL BE MADE UP TO US a hundred fold,[16]
and one day He will personally
WIPE AWAY ALL OUR TEARS.[17]

Yes, God will make everything right in the end, but in the meantime, He can help us learn, grow, and become more like Him through our painful experiences.

IF WE INVITE HIM, HE WALKS WITH US EVERY STEP OF THIS JOURNEY AND HELPS US LEARN FROM THE OPPOSITES OF THIS WORLD.

A few years ago, one of my best friends growing up died from bone cancer. A day or two before Brent passed away, we sat on the edge of his bed and relived all of our favorite memories. There was the time at camp when we threw water on a nest of spiders that was above our Scout leader's head. There was the other time when we tied empty Coke cans to fishing line and strung it across the road so that passing cars would drag the cans behind them. We got chased for a solid two blocks and had to hide behind a mattress in his garage to avoid getting caught. One night at 2:00 a.m. my other friend Rob and I prank called Brent's own house and handed the phone to him without him knowing we had dialed his dad's number. He was so confused when his dad said his name from the other line.

"Brent?!"

"Dad!?"

We had a great childhood. We rode bikes to Target, built tree houses behind the levee, went swimming in the golf course lakes, and ate mountains of Otter Pops in the summers. We graduated high school, went to college, went on missions, and were both married to darling women in the temple. We had the best memories.

Knowing that a goodbye was coming, I took the chance to tell Brent how much he meant to me. I told him that he had always been a really good friend to me and how much I loved him. Then I thanked him for watching out for me.

"Brent," I said, "I always knew if I was with you, I would never be in trouble."

He looked over at me with thoughtful eyes and then said, "Dave . . . I can't say the same about you." We laughed deep belly laughs. It was true. I was the mischievous one. The spider stunt was my idea. Brent got blamed.

A few days later, I spoke at Brent's funeral. I retold some of those same memories. I cried really hard that day. There have been several days since then that I have cried about losing Brent so early. That was one of the hardest things I have experienced in my life so far. It was so unexpected and it seemed so unfair. I really miss him.

After the funeral, Brent's wife, Kelly, gave me a gift from him. It was two framed pictures. One of them was a picture of me and Brent, which I treasure.

The other was a framed quote:

"No pain that we suffer, no trial that we experience is wasted. It ministers to our education, to the development of such qualities as patience, faith, fortitude and humility. All that we suffer and all that we endure, especially when we endure it patiently, builds up our characters, purifies our hearts, expands our souls, and makes us more tender and charitable, more worthy to be called the children of God . . . and it is through sorrow and suffering, toil and tribulation, that we gain the education that we come here to acquire and which will make us more like our Father and Mother in heaven."

—Orson F. Whitney[18]

Every part of this world, especially the hard ones, has the ability to train us and tutor us and turn us into something wonderful. This is a lesson that Brent learned through his own trials. It is a lesson he believed. And so did James who got the sword, and Peter who got the angel, and the other Peter who got the sword that turned into an angel, and so did that prisoner who wrote his own testimony on the wall of a prison.

"I BELIEVE
in God
EVEN WHEN
He is silent."

And it is a lesson I believe too.

9

COMMANDMENTS, JUSTICE, AND LAWS, *OH, MY!*
GOD SHOWS HIS LOVE THROUGH HIS JUSTICE

Every time I got in my car in Mexico, my friend Emily reminded me forcefully to go the speed limit. We were there together on a humanitarian trip and she knew that I was not the best rule keeper—especially on the roads. So she warned me about the police every single time we drove somewhere. She told me horror stories of American tourists who get held back or pay enormous fines or spend the night in jail. I thought her warnings were silly and an overreaction until I saw the flashing lights in my rearview mirror on some coastal highway south of the border. I was certain this was going to end with a tour of the Tijuana prison system. The situation was sort of a mess. Neither of the police officers spoke English, and the only words I know in Spanish are "stupid," "crazy," "goodbye," and "Where is the library?" I didn't think any of those would help my case, unless of course they loved books and thought getting to the library was a justifiable reason to speed. I had three of my kids with me as well and did not know what to do. I should've listened to Emily's advice. I decided to just keep my mouth shut and smile as the officers searched the car and asked me questions that I just cheerfully nodded my head to. Finally, and luckily, they said some parting words and headed back to their car. They let me off the hook. No ticket. No jail. And no more speeding.

As I drove away from my mini Mexican miracle, I had an interesting thought. Usually, if police officers let you go without giving you a ticket (even though you were guilty of speeding), you call them good cops. You like them. If they uphold the law (like they are paid to do) and give you a ticket for your crime, you drive away upset with them, mumbling under your breath about what bad cops they are. In reality, if they actually are doing their jobs, that would make them good. If they let criminals go free, that would make them bad. For some reason, most of us don't see it this way. We are only concerned about whether their actions benefit us. Many of us feel the same way about other law enforcement, teachers, and sometimes parents. If they are lenient, we call them good. If they stick to the rules, no one likes them. Unless of course it benefits us for them to stick to the rules!

Rules, laws, commandments, and justice are not ideas that we normally associate with love. We want a merciful, lenient, and compassionate God. And we have one. But we also have a just God, and that is another manifestation of His love. Heavenly Father is a rule keeper.

He is strictly true to His word.

He upholds all the laws of eternity and follows through perfectly on everything He says. This is being just. The law of justice is the unchanging law that brings about consequences for all actions—bad AND good.

God upholds the law of justice 1OO PERCENT OF THE TIME. And we want Him to. Can you imagine living in a world where there were no absolutes and no guarantees? What if God kept changing the rules? What if we never knew what He was going to do? What if He changed His mind when He had a bad day or just because He felt like it? Is that a God of love? Is that a God you would want to worship? Everything would be chaos.

Think about this:

What is one thing God will never change His mind about
that you are happy for?

God is unchanging.

EVERY **PROMISE** HE HAS EVER MADE OR WILL MAKE IS **CERTAIN**. EACH AND EVERY ONE OF HIS WORDS WILL COME TO PASS.

This includes all of the blessings He has promised you. This is a truth the Lord taught us in the Doctrine and Covenants.

"There is a law, irrevocably decreed in heaven before the foundations of this world, upon which all blessings are predicated—And when we obtain any blessing from God, it is by obedience to that law upon which it is predicated" (D&C 130:20–21).

Irrevocably means that there is no chance that it will not happen. Otherwise, God would cease to be God. That is how certain you can be that He will bless you according to His promises. You can feel safe and secure with every word He has ever said.

God is unchanging, and we **want** Him to be. He **keeps** all of His **laws**. His **motives** for His laws are **always for our good**.

Joseph Smith taught that God

"never will institute an ordinance or give a commandment to his people that is not calculated in its nature to **promote that happiness** which he has designed, and which will not end in the greatest amount of good and glory."[19]

➤———→

Pick any of God's commandments.
How does **keeping** that commandment lead to **happiness?**

_____

Parents and teachers and other leaders are not always like that. We have a bedtime at our house. It partly exists for the happiness of the kids, but it is mostly for my happiness as the dad. I want to get some stuff done. And by stuff I might sometimes mean Netflix. Curfew is similar. It is mostly designed to protect my kids, but it is definitely partly designed so I don't have to worry and can go to sleep. Many of my dad rules are designed, at least in part, for my own happiness.

Heavenly Father's laws and commandments, however, are specifically and completely designed to bring about *our* eternal
happiness and good. None of God's commandments were for Himself. That is not
what He is like.

HE HAS NO SELFISH
MOTIVES IN HIS LAWS.

He has no Netflix shows to get to.

There are some people that say God would be more loving if He
just let us do what we wanted. Get rid of punishment. Get rid of the
laws. These people do not understand that the laws of God *are* His
love. Getting rid of laws means we get rid of God's promises and
blessings to us. It also gets rid of our choices to be happy. We are
naturally happier when we obey eternal laws. THAT iS THE WAY THiNGS
ARE. All laws have a blessing for obeying and a penalty for disobey-
ing. That is what makes a law a law. If we get rid of punishment,
then we lose laws. If we lose laws, we lose the blessings and chance
for happiness, too.

God does not want us to experience the consequences of bad
choices, but He does not and will not get rid of them, either.
HE LOVES US TOO MUCH TO DO
THAT. Instead, God promotes, inspires, and tries to encourage
us with all of His energy to obey these laws. He knows that they will
help us to reach our divine potential. He will not, however, force us
to obey them.

GOD KNOWS
the **best**
choice for us,
but He does **not force**
our hands.
≡ INSTEAD, ≡
He
tries
to win
OUR HEARTS.

There are times when my kids love to jump from bed to bed or couch to couch in some invented game. Little kids have zero coordination, and there is a trip to the ER or a concussion waiting every time they want to play "the floor is lava" in the living room. I warn them again and again to stop or they are going to get hurt. They never listen. They just keep jumping back and forth. The game is way too fun, and they are clueless about how they could possibly get hurt. I get upset with them for not listening to me—not because I want to be the boss, but because I don't want them to get hurt or to hurt someone else. Finally, in frustration, I will usually yell that I don't care if they get hurt and when they do I will not be sad. Again, there is usually no response. But, between you and me, this is a bald-faced lie. I do care and I am sad every time they get hurt.

And even though they were disobedient, I still run to help when the accident happens. And if someone was at fault, that child receives an additional consequence. The child will never learn otherwise.

If an imperfect dad like me gets sad and is still willing to help even though my children disobey,

imagine what our perfect Father in Heaven is like.

He warns us about the consequences of bad choices.

He is like the dad calling from the kitchen warning us that we will get hurt. Sometimes He is extremely firm in His warnings and has to use His angry voice because He knows how dangerous our choices can be. Kids usually hear the angry voice and interpret it as mean—but it is used out of love.

GOD'S ANGER IS A MANIFESTATION OF HIS CARE.

He gets angry when we hurt each other. This is because of how much He loves all of His children. Remember the robber who pointed a gun at my friend in the last chapter? No doubt God was upset with him. This is because He loves my friend—and the robber. Anytime a person commits a crime against another person, there is a punishment. That punishment shows the value God has for the feelings of the victims—people who were hurt. He also has feelings for the sinner. This concern is what makes Him upset with them. Not only do they hurt others, but they hurt themselves. When my kids eventually crash into each other and start crying, I get upset. I am upset they are hurt *and* I am upset that they didn't listen and prevent it from happening. THAT IS WHAT LOVING PARENTS ARE LIKE. Breaking God's laws hurts us spiritually. And when we break His commandments, it breaks His heart. He knows that we cannot actually break eternal laws; WE ARE THE ONES WHO END UP BROKEN. And when we are broken and need Him, He still comes to us—even if we are broken from our own disobedience. He never says, "I told you so!" But as sad as He is, He still does not erase the laws and punishments.

Outside many courthouses is a statue that represents justice. It is usually a woman that is blindfolded and is holding a sword of punishment in one hand and a set of scales in the other. Like all scales, when you add weight to the plate on one side, it goes down and the other side goes up. The weight puts it out of balance. In order to get the plates back even with each other, you would need to put an equal amount of weight on the other side. The scales are usually called the scales of justice. When someone commits a crime, it has to be balanced out with a punishment that is equal in weight to the crime that was committed. That is the only fair way to have a good society. That is the only way to show victims that they are loved and that they matter. Everyone agrees with this, except for the criminal. No one wants dangerous speeders on the roads. They should be punished for putting everyone else at risk. But if you are the speeder, you want the police to let you go for free. That is why the woman is normally blindfolded. People say that justice is blind. When the lady of justice gives her punishment to balance out the scales, she does it only based on the crime, not on the person. Justice does not care what you look like, how you are dressed, how much money you have, or who your friends are. Punishments balance out the crimes for everyone.

What is the purpose of **coming to earth?**

_____

What is the purpose of **laws?**

_____

What would **happen** if you got rid of laws?

_____

Keeping a law leads to _____

_____

Breaking a law leads to _____

_____

Even though we do not like punishments, we would never want to get rid of the law of justice or any of God's laws. This is one of the great ways that God shows His love. The laws God has orchestrated and upholds allow Him to bless us and help us to become like Him. His anger and punishments show how much He cares about our feelings and how desperately He wants us to be happy. We want God to be fair. We want Him to be just. But for those of us who speed down Mexican highways, or jump from couch to couch in a game of lava, we want there to be another way. As we make mistakes on the highway of life or hurt our brothers and sisters, we wish there were another way to balance out the scales. And there is.

IT'S ANOTHER WAY GOD SHOWS HIS LOVE.
IT'S ANOTHER ONE OF HIS LAWS.

It's called the law of mercy.

10

SECOND CHANCES
GOD SHOWS US LOVE THROUGH THE LAW OF MERCY

The Calls were one of the best parts about serving in the Korea Seoul West Mission. They were the senior couple that served in the mission office while I was there. I adore them. One morning, Elder Call came downstairs to the office and said, "Elders, I have a question for you. Do you WANT GOD TO BE FAIR WITH YOU ON JUDGMENT DAY? Think about it." Then without waiting for an answer, he took off his tweed old-man hat and long tan coat, hung them on the hook, and headed into his office. We all looked at each other in confusion. Initially I thought he was scolding us for something we had done wrong. I started to scan my memories of the previous few days. *Had I said something mean to his wife? Did we forget someone or something?* By midafternoon, though, I had switched my way of thinking. I decided to actually ponder the question.

WHAT DO YOU THINK?
DO YOU WANT GOD TO BE FAIR WITH YOU ON JUDGMENT DAY?

 YES. No.

EXPLAIN:

_____

As I walked down the icy street, I began to wonder if I wanted God to be fair with me on Judgment Day. At first I thought—yes! I love fairness. Everyone should be fair. God is fair. God is just. But then I remembered what that would actually mean. If God is fair with me on Judgment Day, it means that I get what I deserve. Considering the choices I make from day to day and the commandments and laws I break with professional status, I did not want to get what I deserved. I did not want God to be fair with me on Judgment Day. I do want God to be fair, just not with my sins. With those I want Him to be merciful.

Like we talked about in the last chapter, God is certainly fair and just. That is a manifestation of His love. His justice allows us to progress and become like Him. Eternal law makes us happier. It is when we break the laws that we have trouble. At times, the justice of God makes people think He is mean. What this really means is that they wish there were another way to balance the scales of justice. They want His love to overpower His laws. What they really want is leniency, not love.

BUT GOD iS LAWFUL AND LOViNG.

He is just and merciful.

HE IS FAIR AND FORGIVING.

THROUGH JESUS CHRIST, GOD OFFERS US A NEW LAW TO OBEY.

Through the Atonement of Christ and the gospel of Christ, the Father introduced the laws of faith and repentance that allow Him to stay a just God AND be merciful. We want God to be a God of justice, but justice required that every broken law have a punishment. Jesus paid the penalty of the broken law for us and balanced out the scales. Through the gospel law of repentance made available through Jesus Christ, WE CAN CHOOSE TO ACCEPT JESUS' PAYMENT FOR US AND BECOME CLEANSED AND ENTER INTO OUR FATHER'S PRESENCE. God will never go back on His promises about repentance and second chances. That is also justice. The gift that He and His Son offered to us allows God to maintain His just laws and still manifest His merciful and compassionate nature as well.

Throughout scripture, we see both the loving law of justice and the loving law of mercy. Sometimes you see one more clearly than the other. Have you ever read the Old Testament? It has to be one of the wildest books in the world, and probably one of the most misunderstood. Most people come away with an unpleasant and unfair summary—floods, man-eating whales, fireballs from heaven, walls tumbling down, and she-bears coming out of the woods to eat children. Yikes! I got a call one time from a friend who asked me,

"DID GOD GET NICER IN THE NEW TESTAMENT?"

Over the years, I have had several students and friends ask me similar questions—questions that center on the character and nature of God. I am so glad every time someone asks me questions like that. It gives me one more chance to praise the Father and change the person's thinking about the NiCEST BEiNG iN THE UNiVERSE. There are certainly times in the Old Testament when God seems to be filled with only justice. He is a God who punishes the wicked in the Flood and in Sodom and Gomorrah. To understand those times we want to remember our last chapter about how the justice of God shows His love. We also want to remember that the God of the Old Testament is also the God who opens the Red Sea and closes the lions' mouths for Daniel.

GOD SHOWS US HIS LOVE THROUGH JUSTICE AND MERCY.

One of the most well-known and loved stories from the Bible is the parable of the prodigal son. You might remember this parable. It's a story about a rebellious boy who leaves home with his father's money, spends it all in wickedness, and then returns home looking for forgiveness and second chances.

Did you know that Jesus didn't name most of His parables? Bible readers and scholars gave them names based on what they are about. The popular name for this parable, "The Prodigal Son," unfortunately takes the attention off of one of its central messages—the character of the Father.

For a long time I thought I knew what the word *prodigal* meant. I thought it meant repentant or sorrowful or rebellious—and it can mean those, in some conversations. However, I looked it up and learned that its first definition is "RADICALLY EXTRAVAGANT." Being prodigal means that you are going over the top with something. All out! You know how little kids go crazy with sprinkles on their ice cream? Yep. They are prodigal with their sprinkles. Get it?

So in the story, the son is definitely prodigal. He is extravagantly wasteful. He spends all of his father's inheritance. A prodigal spender!

But what about the father? How is he radically extravagant? Does the new title of "The Prodigal God" match the story?

{ "A CERTAIN MAN HAD TWO SONS: AND THE YOUNGER OF THEM SAID TO HIS FATHER, FATHER, GIVE ME THE PORTION OF GOODS THAT FALLETH TO ME. AND HE DIVIDED UNTO THEM HIS LIVING" (Luke 15:11–12). }

In the culture of the day, what the son had just asked for would be worthy of a paddling or perhaps getting kicked out of the house. It was overly rude and disrespectful. You only received an inheritance when your father died—never early. And it was the father who had earned it in the first place and gave it as a gift at his own cost. What the son was essentially saying was, "I wish you were dead. I never liked you. I only wanted your money." A slap in the face!

The first shocking part of the story—especially for those who understood and lived in that culture—is the fact that the father doesn't kick the kid out of the house but actually gives him the money. He sells his land and part of "his living" to give it to the undeserving boy. Can you imagine how the father felt? He must have given up a part of his wealth, reputation, lifestyle, and respect in the community to honor the bratty wishes of a rebellious boy.

And off the son went to waste it all in riotous, prodigal living. One weekend on the ancient equivalent of the Vegas strip and it was all gone. So he was forced to beg and eat with the pigs. He hit rock bottom. And then, lying in a muddy pigpen, the boy "comes to himself" and thinks of a plan!

"And when he came to himself, he said, HOW MANY HIRED SERVANTS OF MY FATHER'S HAVE BREAD ENOUGH AND TO SPARE, AND I PERISH WITH HUNGER! I will arise and go to my father, and will say unto him, Father, I have sinned against heaven, and before thee, and am no more worthy to be called thy son: make me as one of thy hired servants" (Luke 15:17–19).

Would you let the boy come back home? Would you give him a job and let him work for you after what he had done? What do you learn about the dad by the fact that the boy even considered it a possibility not only to show his face back on the family farm but to get hired to work?

Back to the story. The boy started to present his apology and plan for making up for his mistakes, but he was interrupted by an unexpected response from his father.

"And he arose, and came to his father. But when he was yet a great way off,

HIS FATHER SAW HIM,
AND HAD COMPASSION, AND RAN,
AND FELL ON HIS NECK, AND KISSED HIM.

And the son said unto him, Father, I have sinned against heaven, and in thy sight, and am no more worthy to be called thy son.

"But the father said to his servants, BRING FORTH THE BEST ROBE, AND PUT IT ON HIM; AND PUT A RING ON HIS HAND, AND SHOES ON HIS FEET: And bring hither the fatted calf, and kill it; and let us eat, and be merry" (Luke 15:20–23).

The story says that the father came to meet his son when "he was yet a great way off." How would the father have known the boy was coming? How would he know unless he had been watching from the window? Waiting. I imagine his wife asking him night after night if he wanted to come to the table for dinner.

"No, thank you," perhaps he would say. "I will just eat here by the window."

"Honey, it is cold. Come closer to the fire."

"No. Not tonight," would be his reply. "I will just take an extra blanket. I AM WATCHING FOR MY BOY."

And when that boy came over the hill dressed in dirty rags and smelling like pigs, I can picture the father leaping up, his chair toppling over, feet scrambling and running with recklessness to meet him.

In those days, fathers didn't run. Little kids ran. Even some teenagers ran. But never men. It was beneath an owner of an estate to do something like that. Those neighbors would have been talking! And the father would have happily taken attention off of his embarrassed son by running past them all.

When he saw his son, he couldn't help it. LOVE SPILLED OUT OF HIS HEART and went right into his legs. He scooped up his robes from around his sandals and booked it out of the house, leaving a trail of dust as he ran to embrace his son in a COMPASSIONATE COLLISION!

Did you notice that the hugs and the kisses came before the boy ever opened his mouth? NO APOLOGY. NO BEGGING. NO EXPLANATIONS CAME BEFORE THE FATHER FORGAVE. The boy tried to plead his case. He explained his unworthiness to be a son and started to lay out his plan to earn his way back into the family, but the father wouldn't have it.

"Bring the robe!
Bring the shoes!
Bring the best ring!
Kill the fatted calf!
You, my boy, will not buy your way back into this family.
You will not earn your place. It will be given to you!"

Whose robe and ring and shoes do you think they were?

And the fatted calf? That was reserved for the most special of occasions. Not even the favorite daughter would get the fatted calf at her engagement party. It was one of the father's most treasured assets. The father's most prized possession would die to bring the boy back into the family. And the boy would come back not as a servant, but as a son, wearing a royal robe and ring.

Break down the parable.

What do all of these **represent** or look like in *your life?*

The father: _____

_____

The rebellious boy: _____

_____

The return of the boy back home: _____

_____

The father running to him: _____

_____

The robe, ring, and fatted calf: _____

_____

_____

This parable shows us a perfect picture of the Father—our

KINDEST, MOST FORGIVING, EXTRAVAGANTLY MERCIFUL, AND RADICALLY ADORING FATHER.

This is what His heart has always been like—even during the Old Testament. God doesn't get nicer in the New Testament, because He has always been merciful. He wants you and me to receive the better end of the deal. He offers His love and His mercy to us in so many ways—in every way that He can and that we accept. HE ANXIOUSLY WAITS FOR OPPORTUNITIES TO POUR OUT GOODNESS ON US AS HIS CHILDREN. Certainly there would have been a conversation between the father and the son about the son's choices and the future consequences of those. There were lessons to be learned and repentance to be done.

Arising from the pigsty is never easy, but when we need help, HE COMES RUNNING. When we need love, HE FILLS US TO OVERFLOWING. The day should never come when we stop being amazed at how good and COMPASSIONATE He is.

When we see HIS MERCY as it truly is, it will be overwhelming and shocking. When you can't see it, you can assume it, because IT IS ALWAYS HAPPENING behind the scenes.

God is a merciful God. It is one of the ways He shows His love. As Elder Jeffrey R. Holland once taught, "Surely the thing God enjoys most about being God is THE THRILL OF BEING MERCIFUL, especially to those who don't expect it and often feel they don't deserve it."[20]

When is a time that God has shown you mercy?

_____

_____

_____

_____

_____

A few years ago I came into my bedroom and found a note sitting on top of my pillow with a simple "Dear dad" written on the front with green marker. It was in the cutest seven-year-old's handwriting, with a backwards "e" in the word "dear." I went over and picked it up. It was a collection of small papers torn out of a little notebook and then stapled together down the side to make a new little booklet. I turned the "Dear dad" page to start reading. There were just a few short sentences on each page—all in that same darling handwriting. I flipped through the note and this is what it said:

"Dear dad,

what happened was this. I took your laser pointer to school today and now I can't find it. It must have fallen out of my backpack when I pulled out my lunchbox. Tomorrow I will go to the front office and I will search down all the hallways to see if I can find it. If I can't, I will do extra jobs around the house to earn the money to buy you a new one. I am so sorry.

Love, jack."

And then the part that tugged on my heart.

"p.s. can you ever forgive me?"

I started to cry immediately. Jenny wondered what was wrong, so I handed her the note to read for herself.

When she was done, I turned to her and said, "I just learned for the first time in my life why God is so forgiving. IT'S BECAUSE HE IS A FATHER. And when his little boys or girls come to Him looking for help or forgiveness or mercy, it is not a criminal talking to a judge, but it is a precious child coming to his or her dad." I went right into Jack's room and just squeezed him so tight I thought his eyeballs might pop out. Of course I forgave him. There wasn't even another option.

If you are ever in need of a second chance, remember this:

Your Father is **watching** for you out the window.

HE HAS **SAVED HIS BEST** ROBE AND RING **FOR YOUR RETURN.**

He has killed the fatted calf and **prepared** the celebration.

In love He lets you sit in the pigsty a while, but the moment you come up over that hill, He will run to you and meet you with a giant, squeezing hug.

HIS **MERCY** IS PRODIGAL.
IT IS WHAT YOU CAN EXPECT EVERY TIME.
SO COME HOME.
YOUR FATHER IS WAITING.

11

TENDER MERCIES
GOD SHOWS HIS LOVE THROUGH CONSTANT AND CONSISTENT CARE

Once upon a time there was a dad who blew it. It was me. It was the Sunday morning of stake conference and we pulled up to the church building only ten minutes late. The snow was falling with a vengeance and the parking lot was a train wreck. Everyone was parked in random diagonal directions and there were piles of snow at every entrance. My sister-in-law Jessie was in town with her kids, so between the three adults that were there we had nine million children under the age of six. We started sloshing toward the front door, walking in between cars with flashing hazard lights, shielding our faces from the brutal blizzard. I had a baby in each arm and one holding onto my suitcoat jacket like a leash when my son Christian stopped in the middle of traffic with a panicked look.

"Oh no! I lost my Lego sword!"

Somewhere between the van and the sidewalk of the church he had dropped the sword to his pirate Lego man that he had insisted on bringing with him to the meeting. I stopped just long enough for my socks to become saturated with icy slush, glanced around at the muddy, messy foot-and-a-half of parking lot snow, gave up hope, ignored his cry, and then hurried them all over the curb and into the church.

"But what about my sword?" Christian pleaded.

"Buddy," I said, "there is no way you can find that sword."

Just as the words left my mouth an impression came to my mind.

Just pray to find it. GOD KNOWS WHERE IT IS.

Then I backpedaled. What if He doesn't answer? Then Christian will start to doubt and think that God doesn't care. I can't risk it.

Then it got worse. Christian had had the same idea.

"Can't we just pray to find it?" Christian asked with believing eyes.

"Chrischi," I started, taking one more look at the blizzardy mess that I could have easily lost a child in. "That sword is lost forever. There are some things even God can't find."

I think that was the moment I won my very first Dad of the Year award.

Two hours later, after successfully winning the wrestling match we call church, we started making our way back out into the tundra. Just as you might have guessed, as we walked back through the freezing slop that every car in our stake had driven through, Christian let out a cheer and held up the sword between his little fingers in victory.

"I found it!"

"What!?" I turned in shock. "How did you do that? Where was it?" I asked. I seriously couldn't believe it.

"I prayed, Dad. I prayed and then I found it. I guess you were wrong. Heavenly Father did know where it was."

Yep. That's when I won my second Dad of the Year award. You get two for particularly brilliant parenting strategies like that one.

Christian bounced back to the car dripping with slush and faith. I walked back with wet socks.

I guess I was wrong. So I am here to set the record straight. God not only knows where lost Legos are, but He cares about them too. Especially when it is one of his darling children who has lost one. He cares about lost keys and lost wallets, too. HE ESPECIALLY CARES ABOUT LOST SOULS.

One of the ways God shows His love to us is in His constant care and interaction with us. He did not create the world, start spinning it in its orbit, send us down, and then move on to other things. HE INTENDED TO PARENT US EVERY DAY OF OUR JOURNEY. Yes, life experience would help us learn, but He is the One who actually does the teaching. He wants to hear from us and wants to speak to us consistently and constantly. This is why He teaches us to pray. It is our way of speaking with Him.

There are lots of reasons people pray.

HABiT.   Avoiding guilt.   To BE GooD.

To ask for help.   BECAUSE WE ARE "SUPPOSED TO."

Some nights it is one of those reasons, and some nights another. And some nights we don't pray at all. And why not?

Perhaps we feel like we don't need it. Perhaps it has become routine and has lost some of its majesty. Perhaps we feel unworthy. Remembering who God is and our relationship with Him begins to tackle all of these problems.

We can **talk to God** wherever and whoever we are.

WALKING. KNEELING.

SAINT. SINNER.

Anytime, Anywhere, Anyone.

THERE IS NO WRONG WAY TO PRAY.
JUST PRAY.

Don't let the devil tell you otherwise.

YOU ARE A CHILD SPEAKING TO A FATHER, NOT A CRIMINAL TALKING TO A PAROLE OFFICER OR JUDGE.

Spill your heart. Your weaknesses. Your sins.
Your fears. Your favorite memories of the day. Your wishes.

YOUR HOPES.
EVERYTHING.

There isn't anything He doesn't want to hear about.
And He is available 24/7.

I recently saw on Instagram a series of pictures from a friend of mine. The first one was of a flat tire on her car early one morning. The sun was not even up and it was icy and freezing outside. The next picture was of her dad jacking up the car to change the tire. There aren't many peo-ple you have permission to wake up and ask for help from on a morning like that one. But dads are on that short list. Our Father in Heaven, too, is there.

True prayer lets you ENJOY MOMENTS iN HEAVEN. In its purest form, it is CONNECTING WiTH OUR FATHER. It is coming home. It is not checking off boxes; it is checking in. It is about a relationship, not a routine. It is spending time with Him—time He is anxiously waiting to spend with you. You know how thrilling it is when you receive an answer to prayer? When you feel like God has made contact with you?

The thrill you feel when He reaches down is the same thrill He feels when you reach up.

Oh, how He misses you.

We can tell Him our struggles. We can thank Him for His goodness. We can ask Him for advice. We can just vent. He is the best listener, and you won't find a better secret keeper. He cares about all of it! He won't get distracted or put you on hold.

As Elder Neal A. Maxwell taught,

"GOD HAS NO DISTRACTING HOBBIES OFF SOMEWHERE IN THE UNIVERSE. WE ARE AT THE VERY CENTER OF HIS CONCERNS AND PURPOSES."[21]

Let Him cheer you on in your victories and in your failures. Lean on Him. Get to know Him by talking to Him. These private conversations you have together are pure gold. Don't just say your prayers. Actually pray.

Praying is not a requirement. Praying was not made up by prophets. Our Heavenly Father has always asked us to pray. The invitation—the plea—came from Him. HE WANTS TO SPEAK WITH US (see Alma 34:18–27; 37:36–37).

I realize that not all stories end so happily and not all prayers are answered so dramatically as Christian's Lego prayer. But whatever the outcome, God does hear and care about every single prayer we offer. That is because HE HEARS AND CARES ABOUT EVERY SINGLE ONE OF US. He is compassionate in His giving and He knows exactly what to give. He knows how to raise His children to be the happiest they can. There are times when we feel like He is not hearing and answering our prayers. In fact, there are problems that I have been praying about for more than fifteen years that I still don't have answers to. You will have those too. But just because He doesn't answer the way we want doesn't mean He won't answer, and it certainly doesn't mean He didn't hear it or care about it.

If we knew what He knows, and loved how He loves, we would answer our prayers the very same way.

Some might wonder why Heavenly Father asks us to pray in the first place. If He already knows what we need and want, why are we going through the hassle? Because God is not Amazon Prime or a butler; HE IS A FATHER. He wants to be in communication with us. In these times of prayer, our hearts change. They change with asking and pleading. That is why He has us ask and plead.

THE TIME WE SPEND iN HiS PRESENCE iS PART OF THE GiFT.

So when we pray for a long time for something, we are spending a long time with Him. If we are patient, He will teach us things and we can be changed through the time we are waiting for and wanting something. My friend once told me that when I can't see the hand of God, I should trust His heart. I know what kind of heart He has, so when He is not intervening when I want Him to or answering the way I hope, I know there is a reason, and that reason will always be love. And even though some of those answers haven't come, HE HAS SHOWN ME THAT HE IS THERE—in little answers and assurances along the way.

What are your prayers like right now?
Where would you put yourself on this scale?

Not
praying
at all

Warm, authentic
communication
with God

What is one way you think you can improve your prayer life?

As often as we are reaching out to Him, He is reaching out to us more often. I loved when Elder Ronald A. Rasband taught that "what may appear to be a random chance is, in fact, overseen by a loving Father in Heaven. . . . The Lord is in the small details of our lives."[22]

He is moving and working in the details of our lives every single day.

Isn't that thrilling to think about?

Six months before I ever arrived in Korea as a missionary, I went on a trip to New York City with my mom. We had a million minutes of fun—ate at some superb places, went to some fantastic spots, and skillfully evaded a mugging by ducking into a candy shop. It was great!

THEATER TICKET

On one of the nights, we went to an off-Broadway show called *The Fantasticks*. Neither of us had ever heard of it before, but we thought, "Hey, let's give it a try."

The play was surprisingly entertaining, and we left the theater looking for dessert, humming the tune to the main song, "Try to Remember," all the way through Times Square. It was a catchy, cute little tune that for better or for worse has still not left my mind.

Six months later I was at a college campus somewhere outside of Seoul, South Korea. My companion and I were not having much success, I could not speak a lick of Korean, and it was still freezing cold even though the calendar said it was spring.

I can still remember standing in the middle of a giant court-yard, picturing a globe in my mind as a heavy realization settled in that I was *literally* halfway across the world. I was frustrated, overwhelmed, and missed home. I thought God had lost me and forgotten where I was. Asia is a big continent, after all, with lots and lots of people.

Interrupting that very sad thought, the loudspeakers on the campus crackled for a moment and then began playing a familiar tune: "Try to Remember."

All at once tears came falling out of my eyes without my permission. GOD WAS PLAYING ME A SONG! In English. At the right moment. Halfway across the world. He just wanted me to know He remembered where I was.

> "SOME MAY COUNT THIS EXPERIENCE AS SIMPLY A NICE COINCIDENCE, BUT I TESTIFY THAT THE TENDER MERCIES OF THE LORD ARE REAL AND THAT THEY DO NOT OCCUR RANDOMLY OR MERELY BY COINCIDENCE."[23]

God is consistently trying to reach out to us, teach us, and take care of us in the best ways. But sometimes it's so subtle we miss it if we aren't looking for it. He sends us friends at the exact time we need them in our life, the perfect sunset on the night we feel alone, the late night conversation that is an answer to prayer, or the song that seems to be played just for you on the radio, at church, or on the Korean college campus. Everywhere we turn, we can see His merciful and tender hand guiding, protecting, and moving in the details of our lives. He is everywhere. In the halls of school, while we are closing at work, in our families, friendships, and conversations. In our brightest days and darkest moments. Everywhere. On a Friday night as much as on a Sunday morning. His love and goodness fill the whole world—your whole world. So look for Him with the same intensity Christian looked for that Lego. IF YOU DO, YOU WILL ALWAYS FIND HIM.

I have left a few blank pages in this chapter for you to try something. An experiment. Over the next two weeks, will you write down one tender mercy or little miracle that you see in your life each day? This may become a pattern of your life—to keep a book of evidences of His love. But for now, I just want you to try it out. Will you??

Tender Mercies

Tender Mercies

12

HIS FAVORED

GOD SHOWS LOVE BY OFFERING MORE

A running joke my brothers and sisters and I all have with each other is a ranking list of who our mom and dad love the most among the kids. Who is the favorite? There are six of us, so we will sit around the kitchen table and each present our arguments for who belongs in each spot—favorite to least favorite. The list is constantly changing. For a while, I was pretty sure I held the number one spot, but I think I dropped in the running when my brother John and sister Jacquelyn both moved their families (and the grandchildren) to Houston, where my mom and dad live. Now it's a fight for third place!

Whenever we joke about it during a family get-together, my mom insists that she loves all of her children equally. Now that I am a dad, I know she is telling the truth. However, if any of my brothers and sisters are reading this, they should know that my birthday text from Mom this year said: "Just wanted to say to my favorite . . . Happy Birthday!"

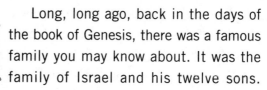

Long, long ago, back in the days of the book of Genesis, there was a famous family you may know about. It was the family of Israel and his twelve sons. The second to youngest son was named Joseph—one you might call Israel's FAVOR-ITE. The writer of Genesis says, "Now Israel loved Joseph more than all his children, . . . and he made him a coat of many colours" (Genesis 37:3). Joseph's brothers were jealous of their father's favoritism and extra love for Joseph. Looks like debating over favorites goes all the way back to the beginning.

One year, while reading through the Bible, I came across this story and wondered whether God had favorites. Sometimes when you look around at others, it may seem like our Father in Heaven is showering down more blessings on certain people and considers them His favorites.

Does He have favorites?

Does He love some of His children more than others? Does He hand out colored coats?

You will be happy to know that the scriptures never use the word *favorite* when talking about the children of God.

HE HAS AN **EQUAL** LOVE FOR ALL OF HIS CHILDREN.

The scriptures do, however, use the phrase "highly favored."

Here are a few people who received this title: **MARY,** the mother of Jesus, was announced by the angel as one who was HiGHLY FAVORED of GOD (see Luke 1:28). The **BROTHER OF JARED** was also called HiGHLY FAVORED of GOD (see Ether 1:34), and **NEPHI** started out the Book of Mormon by saying he was "HiGHLY FAVORED of THE LORD in all my days" (1 Nephi 1:1). What does this mean? How is it different than being a favorite?

There was a city in the Book of Mormon that the prophet Alma went and visited named Ammonihah. It was a wicked city, and he was sent there by the Lord to preach repentance. During part of his visit, Alma reminded the people in the city that they were ONCE A "HiGHLY FAVORED people of the Lord." (Alma 9:20). He seemed to be referring to it as something in the past. Something that had changed. Throughout the next several verses, Alma mentions things that seem to show us what it means to be "highly favored."

Open your scriptures and read Alma 9:20-23.

Highlight or mark different phrases that show what being highly favored means, or write them here.

_____

_____

_____

_____

You may have noticed things like having their prayers answered; being visited by the Holy Ghost and angels; having the gift of prophecy, the testimony of Jesus, and other spiritual gifts; being delivered from their enemies; having God preserve them; and receiving "so many blessings from the hand of the Lord" (Alma 9:21–23).

Hopefully, as you look at this list, you can recognize some of those same favors or blessings in your own life. If not,

YOU SHOULD KNOW THAT EACH AND EVERY ONE OF THEM IS AVAILABLE TO YOU.
GOD GIVES SOME BLESSINGS FREELY AND UNIVERSALLY, AND OTHERS WE NEED TO CLAIM.

The blessing of being "highly favored" is one that we must choose and claim for ourselves, and the choice is available to everyone. God does not just pick favorites.

Long before Alma came, the entire city of Ammonihah was highly favored. It was a status that anyone in the entire city could have. By the time Alma went there on his mission, they had lost that status. IT WAS NOT GOD CHOOSING WHO TO FAVOR——THE CHOICE WAS UP TO THEM, and they had chosen to separate themselves from God. We too get to make our own choices.

God loves all of His children. He loves all of His children universally and infinitely. There are some blessings He pours out upon every one of His children UNCONDITIONALLY just BECAUSE HE iS GOOD and we are His kids. The Resurrection of all mankind because of the Atonement of Jesus Christ is an example of a blessing that God will give to every one of His children. None of us is deserving of it, but HE GiVES iT FREELY. This is true of the Creation of the world and our bodies as well.

In addition to these unconditional blessings, the Father has also promised and invited us to receive MORE of His love and blessings. MORE OF HiS FAVOR. These blessings are equally available to all of His children,

but they must be RECEIVED and ACCEPTED on certain conditions.

President Russell M. Nelson once taught, "While divine love can be called perfect, infinite, enduring, and universal, it cannot correctly be characterized as unconditional. The word does not appear in the scriptures. On the other hand, many verses affirm that THE HiGHER LEVELS OF LOVE the Father and the Son feel for each of us—and certain divine blessings stemming from that love—are conditional."[24]

Brainstorm for a minute about **God's blessings**
that are unconditional and His blessings that are conditional.

UNCONDITIONAL	CONDITIONAL

There is great wisdom in these CONDITIONAL blessings. There may be some who feel that God should pour out all of His blessings on all of His children. They may argue that because of His love, He should bring all of His children back into His presence. Everyone knows someone who gets everything from their parents right when they ask for or demand it. Rarely does that person appreciate it, and often we refer to him or her as spoiled.

·····> GOD IS NOT IN THE BUSINESS OF SPOILING HIS CHILDREN. HE IS IN THE BUSINESS OF EXALTING THEM

(remember Moses 1:39).

He knows what we can become when we choose to obey, follow, choose, and trust Him.

Some of God's blessings and expressions of love can come to us only because of our obedience to His commandments (see John 14:21; 15:10). Throughout the Book of Mormon, the Lord promises that those who are obedient will enjoy an added measure of His goodness: "O remember, remember, my son Helaman, how strict are the commandments of God. And he said: If ye will keep my commandments ye shall PROSPER in the land—but if ye keep not his commandments ye shall be cut off from his presence" (Alma 37:13). This also means there are some who do not enjoy some of the blessings of God's love because of their disobedience. Our Father has INVITED ALL but has also taught us that there are blessings that are dependent on our obedience to His laws (see D&C 130:20–21).

One of these laws that we can obey is the law of repentance. In fact, the greatest of God's blessings can only be claimed by obedience to this law. Forgiveness of our sins, peace of conscience, and the ability to dwell in God's presence are all dependent on us obeying this law. "Therefore only unto him that has faith unto repentance is brought about the great and eternal plan of redemption" (Alma 34:16). Heavenly Father willingly sent His Son to the world to pay the price of our sins, but that is a gift we must receive through repentance.

What are some other **privileges** and **blessings** that God has made available to us that **we must claim** through obedience to His commandments? What must we do to claim them?

BLESSING:	HOW TO CLAIM IT:
Forgiveness of sin	Repentance
Entrance into the celestial kingdom	

God's perfect, infinite, enduring, and universal love is more than we could ever hope to have. It should leave all of us "STAND-ING ALL AMAZED." It is almost unbelievable to know that there is even MORE available to those who choose to accept it. All of His gifts of love are available to all of His children. We might compare some of these conditional blessings to gifts under a Christmas tree. They are purchased, wrapped in beautiful paper, and have our name written on the tag, but unless we CHOOSE to open them, they will stay under the tree waiting. God hopes that we receive all of His gifts, but it is up to us which ones we accept.

IT IS UP TO US TO BE "HIGHLY FAVORED."

I remember coming home from Scout camp one year and seeing my brother John running around in a new pair of shoes. I knew they were expensive, and it had not been his birthday. Why did he get those shoes? It was absolutely and completely unfair. I started out sad and jealous. *I* wanted new shoes. That sadness quickly turned into bitterness and anger. I was certain my parents loved him more and they weren't even trying to hide it. They were playing favorites. Why was John the favorite son?

I spent about a week bottling up my grumpiness until I finally blew. My mom asked me to do a simple chore and I turned on her in a rage. I accused her of loving John more, treating me like the lesser kid, and being an unfair parent. I had proof and I ran with it! When my mom finally got a chance to get a word in, she explained to me that while I was gone at Scout camp (which *she* had paid for), John had scrubbed the tile around the entire pool, scraped the rust off of and repainted the black iron fence, and filled each of his days of vacation doing extra work around the house to earn money for the shoes. John was awake and working from sun up to sun down while I was roasting s'mores around a campfire. THAT IS WHY HE GOT THE SHOES. Sometimes we may look at others and make assumptions about why God is blessing them in the way that He is. We assume He is unfair or picking favorites, when in reality, we just do not know the whole story.

Blessings can and do come from obeying God's laws, but it is important to not misunderstand or demand what some of these blessings should be.

Remember, God is a Father, not a butler.

If we think obeying the commandments is a guarantee of a healthy, long life, we might be disappointed. If we think we will always be blessed by making the team, getting a good job, having our prayers answered the way we want, or making lots of money, we might think we got cheated.

Certainly the Lord can bless people with anything, but the higher blessings He is promising us are not the same as these worldly gifts.

For example, you and your friend might both obey the law of tithing. Your friend might have a really good job, get extra opportunities in the summer, and get to go on an amazing family vacation. You might get stuck with an expensive car repair, lose your job because of hours you can't fit into your schedule, and have to go camping again this year because of a tight family budget. Does this mean that the Lord loves your friend and his family more? Are they being blessed more because of their obedience to the law of tithing? This cannot be true.

God does not love your family any less.

We cannot remember the premortal world, and we cannot see the future. We are never sure exactly what the Lord is doing. We should not make assumptions about the ways He blesses and fulfills His promises. What we can do is look closer at the promises of the Lord. When the "windows of heaven" open, the blessings that come out might be an increase of the Spirit or a spiritual gift we have been seeking (Malachi 3:10).

Perhaps the blessing that comes is simply and beautifully a closer relationship with the Lord. OUR HEAVENLY FATHER KNOWS EXACTLY WHAT WE NEED AND WHAT WE WANT. He is blessing us and loving us in a way that will surprise us with how good He is—even if we cannot see it at first.

It is also important to remember that we do not EARN any of our gifts from God. A gift is a gift. Just because we claim or receive a blessing does not mean we have earned it.

THE GREATEST GIFT our Heavenly Father offers to us is ETERNAL LIFE (see D&C 14:7). This gift is to live with Him eternally in His presence, in a family, with His attributes, perfections, and all that He has. In all of His love, this is the gift He wishes most to give to all of His children. It is a gift He is hoping we will all receive. And He knows exactly how to guide us to it. Sometimes it is through a miracle, and sometimes it is through a trial. Sometimes it is through a certain calling or responsibility, and sometimes it is through an answered prayer or through the invitation to repent. He wants to exalt the President of the Church as much as He wants to exalt a kid slouching in the back of seminary.

All of His greatest blessings are available to all.

This journey will look different for each of us. Some will be poor and some will be rich. Some will be healthy and others will be sick. Some will seem to get all the lucky breaks and others will always end up at the bottom. No matter what the circumstances of our lives look like, He will always bless us in a way that leads us to this end goal. That will always be true. It will require work on our part; this life was never meant to be passive.

Our Heavenly Father will love us whether we choose to be favored or not. He might be disappointed if we don't choose His greatest blessings, but

HE NEVER WILL STOP LOVING US

and will still pour out those universal blessings on us. He will also never stop calling to you or hoping that you will one day receive all of His love. All of His favors. He wants this for all of His children.

There is a colored coat for everyone. And probably a new pair of shoes, too.

We just need to open them and put them on.

13

LOVING GOD BACK

One night while I was putting one of my sons to bed, he looked up at me after he was all tucked in and asked, "Dad, are there Legos in heaven?"

At the time, my son loved Legos. He would play with them all day long, sleep with them, and then first thing in the morning he would hop out of bed and get back to building. He asked for them for Christmas, for his birthday, and every other holiday. In his little mind, heaven would not be heaven without Legos.

I looked back down at him and said, "Of course there are, son. MILLIONS OF THEM."

I am not sure if that is true or not, but he gave me the biggest, most satisfied grin, wiggled back and forth for a second to get a little more snug in the covers, closed his eyes, and whispered, "I knew it. Night night."

For Jackson, the happiest kind of heaven would be a heaven made of Legos. Even though that is not scriptural, the idea of heaven being a place of happiness is (see Alma 40:12). Our Heavenly Father promises us amazing blessings to entice us to choose Him. God's blessings are much more amazing than millions of Legos, but for a three-year-old, that was as good as it gets. It was enough for him! He wanted to go to heaven.

"But as it is written, Eye hath not seen, nor ear heard, neither have entered into the heart of man, the things which God hath prepared for them that love him"

(1 Corinthians 2:9).

We have no idea how wonderful the great blessings of God truly are, but they are promised in their fullness to those who love Him.

The first and greatest commandment that the Lord gave to His children was and is to

"LOVE THE LORD THY GOD WITH ALL THY HEART, AND WITH ALL THY SOUL, AND WITH ALL THY MIND"

(Matthew 22:37).

At first, this might seem like a strange commandment. Why does God command us to love Him? Does He need our love? Certainly not. Does He lose power if we do not adore Him? No. Elder Dieter F. Uchtdorf taught, "God the Eternal Father did not give that first great commandment because He needs us to love Him. . . . No, God does not need us to love Him.

BUT OH, HOW WE NEED TO LOVE GOD!
For what we love determines what we seek.
What we seek determines what we think and do.
What we think and do determines who we are
—and who we will become."[25]

Each of us is iNViTED AND PRiViLEGED to be able to enter into an abiding, fulfilling, and authentic relationship with our Father in Heaven. We can love Him and be assured of His love for us. Throughout the scriptures, you might notice that the Lord will refer to Himself as "your God" and to us as His people (Jeremiah 30:22). This phrase describes a very close relationship. If you heard me talking and I said "my Jenny" or "my Jack," you would assume I was talking about someone that was very close to me. This is the kind of relationship our Heavenly Father hopes we will have with Him.

Where would you put yourself on this scale with your relationship with God today?

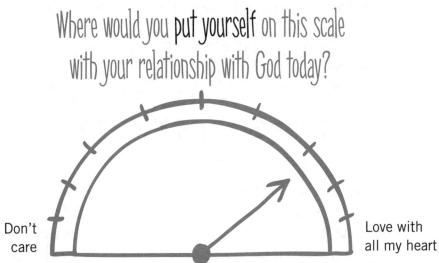

Don't care

Love with all my heart

Here's the good news. Wherever you are, you can always make your relationship better. But where do you begin?

"The perfect place to begin is exactly where you are right now. It doesn't matter how unqualified you may think you are or how far behind others you may feel. THE VERY MOMENT YOU BEGIN TO SEEK YOUR HEAVENLY FATHER, iN THAT MOMENT, THE HOPE OF HiS LiGHT WiLL BEGiN TO AWAKEN, ENLiVEN, AND ENNOBLE YOUR SOUL."[26]

There are many reasons a person would want to seek God. Like it was for my son Jackson, that reason might be to someday live in a Lego heaven. Others might seek God because they want the blessing of eternal families or forgiveness of their sins. There are others who seek God out of fear. They are afraid of hell or punishment if they do not seek Him and obey His commandments. Some of these motivations show a lack of understanding about who God is, and others are wonderful starting points, but the highest motivation and reason to seek God is out of love.

In a letter to the ancient Church, the Apostle John said,

♥ "WE LOVE HIM, BECAUSE ♥ HE FIRST LOVED US"

(1 John 4:19).

As we consider all of the great things our God has done for us, it melts our hearts. We want to trust and love Him. He does not demand our loyalty, but rather He wins it. He shows us His beautiful, divine love and it draws us to Him. Every chapter of this book was written to show how dedicated our Father is to each of us. HE REALLY IS FOR US. We see how good He is and we want to be near Him. Having this type of relationship is one of those highest and most blissful blessings—perhaps it is the highest of all. Just as Jesus, who has this type of relationship with the Father, prayed, "And this is life eternal, that they might know thee the only true God, and Jesus Christ, whom thou hast sent" (John 17:3). Eternal life, the greatest of all the gifts of God (see D&C 14:7), is knowing God and loving God.

Just as John said to the Church members in New Testament times, once we learn about and experience the love of God, we will want to love Him in return. But how do we show love to God?

What could we possibly give Him? He has everything!

Elder Neal A. Maxwell once taught that the only unique thing we really have to give God IS OUR WILL——OUR CHOICES AND LOYALTY. Everything else we have already came from Him, so we would just be returning a gift He already gave.[27]

During ancient times, King David was told by one of the holy prophets to build an altar to the Lord on the property of a man named Araunah. This was a man who was loyal to King David and the kingdom, so when he saw David approaching, he ran out to meet him and bowed down with his face to the ground, offering the king his services and anything else he wanted. When the king told Araunah that he wanted to buy his land in order to build an altar to the Lord, Araunah quickly offered him the land, wood, instruments, and oxen for the sacrifice at no cost to the king. This was a wonderful and very generous offer. However, King David would not accept it.

"And the king said unto Araunah, Nay; but I will surely buy it of thee at a price: neither will I offer burnt offerings unto the Lord my God of *that which doth cost me nothing.* So David bought the threshingfloor and the oxen for fifty shekels of silver" (2 Samuel 24:24; emphasis added).

Even though King David had privileges, discounts, and offers given to him as the royal leader of the land, this was something he did not want to receive for free. He was building an altar to *his* God and King. He did not want his gift to cost him nothing.

IT WAS GOING TO BE HIS WAY OF showing HIS love, loyalty, AND devotion TO GOD. HE WANTED IT TO BE GIVEN AT A COST.

Many years later, David's son Solomon became the king of Israel and was commanded by the Lord to build a permanent temple on the same location. "And the king commanded, and they brought great stones, costly stones, and hewed stones, to lay the foundation of the house" (1 Kings 5:17). I imagine that this is a lesson that Solomon learned from his father. When you build a temple to God, you do it with great stones, costly stones, and hewed stones. Later Solomon would call together all the finest woodworkers, metal workers, and craftsmen to work on the temple.

HE WOULD bring his finest BECAUSE IT WAS FOR HIS GOD.

Sacrifice is a law of love. It shows that we honor something or someone more than ourselves. GOD HAS SHOWN US LOVE THROUGH SACRIFICE, AND IT IS THE WAY WE SHOW OUR LOVE IN RETURN. Like all other relationships we have, coming to know God requires something of us. It requires time, devotion, interest, and trust. It requires us to bring our very finest.

This lesson of bringing your finest is one that I have thought of often. A few years ago I went to Hawaii for my brother-in-law's wedding. Jenny and I were trying to pack light, so we were each only taking a backpack as a carry-on for the plane. As I was packing for the wedding, which was happening in the Laie Hawaii Temple, I realized that my church shoes would take up too much of my bag. There were snacks, books, cards, and other fun things I wouldn't have room for if I took those big, clunky shoes. I went to my closet to switch out my church shoes for my nicest pair of flip-flops. But right when I set down my shoes I thought about David and Solomon. I thought about how they BROUGHT THEIR FINEST. I thought about how LOVE COSTS SOMETHING. I thought about how sacrifice, no matter how great or small, shows our love for a God who has given so much. I put the church shoes back into my bag. HE WAS WORTH IT.

What is one way YOU could sacrifice to show God how much you love Him?

There are many ways we can show this kind of love to God. One of those ways is obedience. OBEDIENCE TO HIS COMMANDMENTS SHOWS HIM THAT WE TRUST HIM. It shows Him that we are choosing Him over the world's way of doing things. When we listen and follow, we show Him how we value His wisdom and His companionship. We seek to listen to His voice and believe that He has our best interests in mind. Again, some might obey Him to avoid a punishment or to receive a reward, but we strive to love and obey Him because of the love He has already shown us. HE HAS PROVEN TO US THAT HE IS DEVOTED TO US. KEEPING HIS COMMANDMENTS IS THE WAY WE SHOW HIM WE ARE JUST AS DEVOTED TO HIM. Interestingly, even though we obey Him to show Him love, He rewards our obedience with even more favor and blessings. In King Benjamin's words, "If ye should serve him with all your whole souls yet ye would be unprofitable servants" (Mosiah 2:21). We could never pay Him back. He doesn't expect us to. HE JUST WANTS OUR HEARTS.

Is there a **COMMANDMENT** you can promise to **ALWAYS** obey to show God your love? What promise can you make today?
➤   To show my love, I will . . .   ◄

We also show Him love by repenting. When we sin or disobey, we essentially tell God that we know how to live our lives better than He does. We take Him off the throne of our hearts and sit in His place.

REPENTANCE

is recognizing that

HE TRULY DOES KNOW BEST,

putting aside our will,

AND INVITING HIM BACK ONTO THE - - - - →

THRONE OF OUR HEARTS.

When we have a repentant spirit, we recognize that we did not just break a commandment, but rather broke His heart. We walked off of His path, offended His Spirit, and hurt Him and others He cares for. When we hurt someone who has loved us so dearly, we want to make things right. When we repent, we show Him APPRECIATION for the greatest gift of His Son. Repentance was the Father and the Son's gift of love to us, but we show love in return by receiving that gift and mending our relationship.

Perhaps one of the best ways we can show love to God is by LOVING OTHERS. Again, in the words of King Benjamin, "When ye are in the service of your fellow beings ye are only in the service of your God" (Mosiah 2:17). When we sacrifice to show love to God's other children, He takes it personally. Serving and loving people is one of the best ways to show our love and devotion to Him.

♥ ♥ ♥ ♥ ♥ ♥ ♥ ♥ ♥ ♥ ♥ ♥ ♥ ♥ ♥ ♥

This week, I will **show love** to God
by showing love to_____
by _____.

♥ ♥ ♥ ♥ ♥ ♥ ♥ ♥ ♥ ♥ ♥ ♥ ♥ ♥ ♥ ♥

There are so many ways that we can show love to a God who has loved us first. As we show Him this love in sincere and authentic ways, it draws us closer to each other and it causes our hearts to become more like His. God has commanded us to love and serve Him with all of our "heart, might, mind and strength" (D&C 4:2). We should remember, though, that everything that He is asking for us to give, He has already given.

HE ALREADY GAVE HIS WHOLE HEART TO US.

When a man and woman decide they want to get married, they not only tell each other that they love each other, but they make promises that they will make their relationship more important than their own personal wants and desires. They promise "YOU OVER ME."

TRUE LOVE IS NEVER SELFISH.
True love is sacrifice.
TRUE LOVE IS DEVOTION.

The best thing we have to offer in any relationship is the best version of ourselves. When both partners make this promise, and fully commit to each other, and live up to that promise, they grow closer to each other in amazing and authentic ways. This can be intimidating. We might be hesitant to make promises to someone if we are unsure that they will make those promises in return. When I was dating in college, my greatest fear was loving someone who didn't love me back. Happily, that will never happen with God. He was the first one to promise and prove that He is fully committed to us. HE LOVED US FIRST. It is our turn to show the same love. If we have to give something up to be close to Him, no matter what it is or however great the cost, it will never come close to the cost that He paid so that He could be close with us.

Throughout our lives, we show our love, our devotion, and our sacrifice and give our finest, and it will bring us closer and closer to each other each day we do. And hopefully, one day, when we meet again (whether it is in Lego heaven or just regular heaven), our reunion will not only be sweet, but also FAMILIAR.

14

TO BE CONTINUED . . .
His Love Keeps on Going

Sometime right before he died, the great Nephite king, Benjamin, wanted his people to gather together so he could share some of his last words and bits of advice. So he had a tall tower built and called the families of the kingdom together to set up tents surrounding it to hear his words. I imagine it being a beautiful morning and the people watching him slowly climb the stairs to the top. I like to picture their faces looking up with anticipation and admiration at a prophet king they loved and respected like a wise grandfather. During his touching goodbye and powerful talk to his people, this is one of the things King Benjamin said:

"Believe in God; believe that **He is**, and that **He created all things**, both in heaven and in earth; believe that **He has all wisdom**, and **all power**, both in heaven and in earth; believe that man doth not comprehend all the things which the Lord can **comprehend**"

(Mosiah 4:9).

Of all the truths the dying king wanted his people to know, at the top of that list was his witness and beliefs about God. Many people reading this book have grown up singing in their living rooms, Primary rooms, and bathrooms (my kids sing it in the tub) that "I am a child of God, and He has sent me here." What a mighty, mighty truth!

I suppose there are some people in the world who imagine that they are just a product of evolution or a random accident from a collision of stars, but I am not one of them. And neither is King Benjamin. Like him, I BELIEVE IN GOD and want to put a list here of things I believe about Him. I probably won't ever read this from the top of a tower, but hopefully I will have the chance to share these truths with people throughout my life. In fact, remember that man who grabbed my hand at the Cheesecake Factory and asked me what I believed? The man with the crooked black hat? After writing this book, I wish I could go back and find him. I wish we could have some time to sit down and talk about God and what I believe about Him. If it were to ever happen, I think I would give him my list—a list that right now looks something like this . . .

There is a God.

He is our Father.

He dwells in the heavens above.

He is an exalted man.

He is married to an exalted woman.

He has a resurrected body of flesh and bones.

He has a name.

He has a personality and preferences.

You are one of His preferences.

You used to live with Him before you were born.

You are His literal child.

You were created in His image.

He raised you.

You knew Him well.

He knew you better.

He is the creator and author of the great plan of salvation.

He sent you here on purpose and with a purpose.

He has eyes to see you with.

Ears to hear your prayers and petitions.

A mouth to speak words of direction, comfort, correction, guidance, and defense.

He can speak with the power of a thousand earthquakes, or with a voice as gentle as a whisper.

He has hands that He holds out.

Hands that He once held you in.

Hands that will embrace you again.

Strong hands. Tender hands.

In His chest is a heart that beats with love and worry for you.

He corrects you when He needs to.

He allows hard things that help you grow.

He lifts you when you fall.

He is patient with you.

He is happy. He is holy. He is everything you hope that He is.

He sees all.

He knows all.

He is over all.

He commands us.

He gives us His laws.

He is the source of all power, all wisdom, all goodness, and all love.

And He can do anything, anytime, anywhere.

There is no problem that is unsolvable and no miracle beyond His ability.

His glory would make your knees knock and your heart skip its beats.

With one word He could alter the universe.

He is Almighty.

He knows you.

He adores you.

He shows those feelings in so many ways.

And you can have a relationship with Him.

Or, rather, rekindle the relationship you already have.

He will always be your loving Father.

You might want to try doing the same thing sometime—make a list about your beliefs. What do you believe about God? How do you see His love? Maybe you want to get out a journal sometime soon and write your own feelings and thoughts about Him. Or you can put it on the blank page I left for you at the end of this chapter. It can start really simple. The most basic truths are usually the most powerful. Perhaps you want to flip through some of the pages of this book again looking for ideas. What have you learned as you have been reading through and thinking about the different chapters? What do you know about Heavenly Father? In what ways have you seen Him in your life?

You and I have been on this earth—this journey God prepared for us and sent us on—for different amounts of time. Some of you less and some of you more. You might not have as many things on your list as I have on mine, or you might have more. Whatever you have, even if it is only two things, they are two very important truths. As we keep living, we will keep adding to our lists.

NEITHER OF OUR LISTS IS DONE.
That's because God's love is never-ending, and He will show up AGAIN and AGAIN in SURPRISING and WONDERFUL WAYS to show that love.

Having a list like this can carry you through the tough times—like it did for Moses. It can help you remember that you have a purpose and a FATHER GOD WHO IS POWERFUL AND LOVING. It can also be a great place to start when people ask you about your beliefs or have questions about Him.

And maybe, just maybe, someday we will run into each other waiting for a table at the Cheesecake Factory. And if it is a long enough wait—which it usually is—we can sit down and talk about a few things. Our beliefs and stories about God. You can share your stories and I can share some more of mine. And all those stories will tell about an

ALMIGHTY GOD
WHO IS ALSO
A LOVING FATHER.

And when we leave, we will add one more story to our list. We will write about the time He brought two of His children together to remind each other about the love of their Father. It would be a coincidence in some people's minds, but in ours we will know it was one more evidence of how good He actually is.

What I believe about God . . .

NOTES

1. See Guide to the Scriptures: "God," "Godhead," "Lord."

2. "I Am a Child of God," *Hymns* (1985), no. 301.

3. *Teachings of Presidents of the Church: Joseph F. Smith* (1998), 335.

4. "Apostasy and Restoration," *Ensign*, May 1995.

5. Eliza R. Snow, *Biography and Family Record of Lorenzo Snow* (1884), 46. The couplet, which has never been canonized, has been formulated in slightly different ways. For others, see *The Teachings of Lorenzo Snow*, ed. Clyde J. Williams (1996), 1–9.

6. "God made man in his own image and certainly *he made woman in the image of his wife-partner.* You [women] are daughters of God. You are precious. *You are made in the image of our heavenly Mother*" (*The Teachings of Spencer W. Kimball* [1982], 25; emphasis added).

7. NOAA, Historical Maps and Charts audio podcast, National Ocean Service website, https://oceanservice.noaa.gov/podcast/july17/nop08-historical-maps -charts.html, accessed on 1/13/18.

8. T. Sharp, "How Big Is Earth?" (September 2017), retrieved from https://www .space.com/17638-how-big-is-earth.html.

9. Andrew Craig, "Astronomers Count the Stars," BBC News (July 22, 2003), http://news.bbc.co.uk/2/hi/science/nature/3085885.stm.

10. "Our bodies are sacred. They were created in the image of God. They are marvelous, the crowning creation of Deity" (Gordon B. Hinckley, "Be Ye Clean," *Ensign,* May 1996).

11. David A. Bednar, "Ye Are the Temple of God," *Ensign*, September 2001.

12. Russell M. Nelson, "Thanks Be to God," *Ensign*, May 2012.

13. See Thomas S. Monson, "I Know That My Redeemer Lives," *Ensign,* April 1990.

14. M. Neeley, "The Family Is of God," *Friend*, October 2008.

15. E. Howe, "I Believe in the Sun, Part 1: Look Away," retrieved from https:// humanistseminarian.com/2017/03/19/i-believe-in-the-sun-part-i-look-away/.

16. "The Lord compensates the faithful for every loss. That which is taken away from those who love the Lord will be added unto them in His own way. While it may not come at the time we desire, the faithful will know that every tear today

will eventually be returned a hundredfold with tears of rejoicing and gratitude" (Joseph B. Wirthlin, "Come What May and Love It," *Ensign*, November 2008).

17. See Revelation 21:4.

18. Orson F. Whitney, quoted by Spencer W. Kimball, in *Faith Precedes the Miracle* (1972), 98.

19. *Teachings of the Prophet Joseph Smith*, sel. Joseph Fielding Smith (1976), 256.

20. Jeffrey R. Holland, "Laborers in the Vineyard," *Ensign*, May 2012.

21. Neal A. Maxwell, "How Choice a Seer," *Ensign,* November 2003.

22. Ronald A. Rasband, "By Divine Design," *Ensign*, November 2017.

23. David A. Bednar, "Tender Mercies of the Lord," *Ensign*, May 2005.

24. Russell M. Nelson, "Divine Love," *Ensign*, February 2003.

25. Dieter F. Uchtdorf, "The Love of God," *Ensign*, November 2009.

26. Dieter F. Uchtdorf, "The Hope of God's Light," *Ensign*, May 2013.

27. See Neal A. Maxwell, "Consecrate Thy Performance," *Ensign*, May 2002.

ABOUT THE AUTHOR

DAVID BUTLER is by day a religious educator sharing his fierce love for the scriptures with anyone willing to listen. By night he is a fort builder, waffle maker, sports coach, and storyteller for his six darling kids. Somewhere in between, he is a motivational speaker and writer. He loves, loves, loves good food, spontaneous adventures, Christmas morning, the first day of summer, and every other day of summer. Above all he loves people. He has chosen as his life motto, "Stuff no mattah. People mattah." He and his adorable wife, Jenny, live with their family amid the snowcapped peaks of the Mountain West, but they often dream of a beach house on a sunny shore somewhere.

 @mrdavebutler